A Theological Reflection on War and Peace

Christian Heritage Rediscovered

The Series, as the name suggests, is meant to focus on Christian Faith & Living vis-à-vis topics like Literature & Poetry, Indigenous Philosophizing, Ethical response towards Agriculture, Health & Healing, Science & Technology, Eco-feminist Theology, Sociological approach towards Human Rights, Law & Politics, Arts, History of Ideas, Ancient Civilizations, Cultural Contiguity, Religious Cosmologies & Mysticism, Footsteps of famous Theologians, World Peace & Harmony, Global Capitalism, Network Marketing, Cybertheology, Population & Demographics, Epigraphic Studies, Contextualized Education, and many others. We welcome a Mss. on any topic/s mentioned, whether they are original works, scholarly monographs, collections of conference papers, revised dissertations, or translations of historical documents. Through the Series we, the Publishers, are striving to put forward published works that may help Institutions, Academic Bodies, Researchers, Scholars and the World at large in furthering their respective knowledge and understanding on the concerned subject. We welcome your comments on our efforts and further suggestions on how we can foster the upcoming thought provoking theologically grounded books.

Christian Heritage Rediscovered - 53

A Theological Reflection on War and Peace

God Never Allows War

L. Seikholen

CWI
Christian World Imprints

First Published in 2019 by

Christian World Imprints
Christian Publishing & Books from India
H-12 Bali Nagar, **New Delhi-110015**
info@christianworldimprints.com
www.ChristianWorldImprints.com
Phone: +91 11 25465925

ISBN: 978-93-5148-205-5 (HB) ISBN: 978-93-5148-206-2 (PB)

Cataloging in Publication Data--DK
Courtesy: D.K. Agencies (P) Ltd. <docinfo@dkagencies.com>

Seikholen, L., 1958- **author.**
A theological reflection on war and peace : God never allows war / L. Seikholen.
pages cm. -- (Christian heritage rediscovered ; 53)
ISBN 9789351482055 (HB)
ISBN 9789351482062 (PB)
1. War--Biblical teaching. 2. Peace--Biblical teaching. 3. Bible--Criticism, interpretation, etc. I. Title. II. Series: Christian heritage rediscovered ; 53.

BS680.W2S45 2019 DDC 261.873 23

Printed in India.

Contents

PART-3

A Theological Reflection on War and Peace

PART-4

Christians' Participation in the Military Service

Preface

It may not be so easy to stop wars between nations by writing and publishing books on war and peace. Books on war and peace in the past might or might not change the world's attitude to war. No religion seemed to condemn war and killing completely. Even Christianity does not have systematic condemnation of war. It is probably true to say that Christianity inherited its positive attitude to war from Judaism or the Old Testament. Thus, writers of the New Testament do not deal with condemnation of war systematically. Since the Old Testament mostly have positive attitude to war, writers of the New Testament too seemed to take for granted that war is an unavoidable evil in the world which cannot be eliminated until the end of the earth.

However, it is also possible to see negative attitude to war in the writings of both the Old Testament and the New Testament. There seems to be a line of thought in the Old Testament too which sharply condemned war and killing. From Genesis to the historical books there are certain passages which really condemned war as an evil. Even the poetical books and prophetic books of the Old Testament have some passages which really condemned war and killings. In the New Testament, it is Jesus who emphasizes non-violence and non-resistance through his teachings, his life and his works. This was not readily understood by Peter, who even used his sword to defend Jesus from his attackers. Even Paul did not make any systematic condemnation of war. It seems true to say that it was Jesus alone who has condemned war as an evil. Although, there hardly is direct condemnation of war in his words, his teachings indirectly show his condemnation of war and killing.

L. Seikholen

Introduction

This book is an attempt to prove that God would never allow human beings to kill or fight as enemies to each other. The book tries to clarify that there are two apposing views on war or killing or violence in the Bible. One view claims that God permits and supports wars between his people and their enemies. This line of thought would sometimes picture God as warrior or even as captain of the army of God (Israel or Judah).

The second view is that God was/is against any act of violence, killing or war. God is always opposed to any kind of ill attitude towards others. Both of these views are made by human beings according to the understanding of the world of that time. Out of these two views the second appears to be much closer to the will of God. In line with this, attempt is made here to prove that God never allows war/killing of any kind between his people.

Some chapters are especially dedicated to deal with passages which have positive view on war. According to the Old Testament, Israelite leaders like Abraham, Moses, judges, kings were taken to accept war as a part of the life of God's people. They all waged war with the view that God not only allows them to fight with other nations, but even joined their wars with other nations as captain of the army of Israel. Some chapters are dedicated to have a critical study of these passages.

A group of chapters are dedicated to point out passages which condemned war or killing in the Pentateuch, the historical books, poetical books, and the prophetical books. Important passages in the New Testament too are chosen to condemn war and killing. These passages, both from the Old Testament and the New Testament, are strong enough to condemn war and killing. The life, teachings and works of Jesus also condemn war and killing.

A good explanation of the Biblical view of God is "Men made God in their own images". The Bible represents human description of God in their own images. In describing God in their own images some writers of the Bible happened to describe God as warrior, captain of the army of Israel. Sometimes some writers used to be closer to God's truth than some writers' presentation of God as warrior, captain of the army, or sometimes asking or allowing Israelites to wage war against their enemies.

This book is an attempt to present/show probable truth that satisfies all open minded theologians. Passages in the Bible which supports God's permission for war are disproved as views of human writers. Passages which oppose war/killing are pointed out as truths similar to God's truth. This is made in line with the view that God is parent of all and would never allow war between His children. All human beings without exception are children of God, and all are brothers and sisters to each other. God loves both the righteous and the sinners, and would never allow wars between them. God loves all and loves sinners too. This is how in the parable of the prodigal son, in which God appears to love the returned prodigal son more than the elder son who was always with the father.

PART-1

A CRITICAL STUDY OF PASSAGES WHICH SUPPORTED WAR/KILLING

There are several passages in the Bible, especially the Old Testament, which supported the view that God supports, permits, and even participates in war, or even leads an army of Israel in war as its captain. God is sometimes described as warrior. Part-1 of this book is dedicated to deal critically with such passages in the Bible.

1

Abraham's War With the Enemies

'Abraham was a man of God. He was nicknamed as the Father of all the Faithful" (Romans 4:16). However, all should agree that all his actions cannot be justified by what he was. God would forgive his weaknesses. However, his war with enemies did not and cannot justify war in general. Although, he was a man of God, his war with enemies cannot be accepted as an example for all. In case of Abraham, he waged war against four kings only because they took captives/prisoners of Abraham's relatives. His war was a different war, because its purpose was only to rescue his relatives. He did not have endless enmity with the enemies.

However, God cannot even justify his (Abraham's) own war with them. Because, there must be possible non-violent means to solve the problem. War is not the right means to solve any problem. Although, Abraham was an example in faith, he had other weaknesses too. Once he told a lie to save himself from the hands of Abimelech and/or Pharaoh in Egypt. Because, he was afraid that he would be killed because of his wife, Sarah. So he said that Sarah was his sister. In order to save his life he betrayed the truth and used his tongue to speak lie. The point taken here is that although he was a man of God, he was not a God and so he could make many mistakes. Some of his actions in his life could be accepted as wrong actions. His war with the enemies was not the right means to rescue his relatives. There must have been other better and non-violent means to rescue his people. However, he chose violent means to rescue his people. It must be a wrong means to deal with people by a man of God.

Our point is that, Abraham was not always right in his choice of actions. Sometimes his actions might have been best examples for the people of God. However, this does not mean that his right actions can justify wrong actions as a norm of life for the people of God. As such, his telling of lie and his war with enemies are results of his wrong choice of actions. His war with the neighbouring kings might have been the way of life of the people around in those days. But they are not acceptable ways of life for the people of God in general.

So, we are right to conclude that Abraham's war with wicked kings does not prove the view that war is acceptable attitude to the wicked world. It is at his weakest point that he chose to wage war against the wicked kings. War cannot simply be justified only because Abraham also fought war against his enemies. Someone would claim that "war was a necessary evil" for Abraham because he needed to save/rescue his people from the hands of evil/wicked kings. This idea may not be applicable or acceptable for those who have the mind to love the wicked. War is never a good solution to problems in the world. It is only weak response to evil. Retaliation belongs to heathens alone. When any man/woman of God committed the sin of retaliation, it is his/her estrangement from God's way. There could have been other means of solution for Abraham, if he could try some other ways.

2

A Study of Moses' Killing an Egyptian

Moses too was a man of God. God is believed to do his works through Moses. However, all his actions cannot be norms for latter people of God, only because of his being a man of God. The fact that "he was used by God" does not guarantee perfection in his actions.

It is true that Moses was a man used by God to do his works. He was especially called by God to lead his people out of Egypt. He was used by God to perform many things in front of Pharaoh. Through him God led Israel out of Egypt. He led Israelites through the Red Sea (or the Reed Sea). He made the Ten Commandments for the people of Israel. He beat the rock of Maribah (Massah) and water came out of it. Through him God gave manna to the Israelites. God use him as he was the man used by God." However, his good works can never justify his actions resulted from his selfish emotion(s). His action of killing the Egyptian was the weak point in his life. It is a dark spot in his life.

It is, therefore, necessary to say that the weak part of the life of Moses cannot be taken as a norm of life for the people of God. Although, he was a man used by God, his killing of a man cannot be an example of perfect life for the whole people of God. Although, he might be one of the best examples for dedicated lives of God's servants, every act of him cannot be an example for the whole people of God. It cannot be an example to be followed by all people of God.

More than that, we can say that wicked actions of human beings can never be accepted as good and acceptable actions simply because the man or woman is a faithful servant of God. God forgives sinners when they are repented. This does not mean that God overlooks sinful actions of sinners. He forgives their sinfulness but never justify sinful actions as if they could be norm of life for God's people. In the same way, although Moses was a man chosen and used by God, his act of killing an Egyptian could not be taken as an action acceptable on the basis of his faith and dedication to God. Therefore, Christians cannot simply say that killing of a wicked man is justifiable by God. Even if one says that killing of a wicked person is justifiable, killing by a man of God, like that of Moses, can never be justifiable. Good people can never have the mind to take revenge, the mind to kill.

As it was the weakest point in Abraham's life to tell lie in order to avoid danger, death, it was a weak point in Moses, to kill an Egyptian only to take revenge. We will see, later, that as Moses was a child of God, so is the Egyptian killed by him, in general?

Even lay Christians can understand the statement that Moses was indeed a man of God, a man used by God. However, this does not mean that God can accept killing as a possible action of Christians, since Moses (a man of God) killed an Egyptian. Moses killed an Egyptian because he could not control his emotional irritation. He fell into the temptation of his emotional outburst. It has happened as a result of his failure to ignore the evil in him that is the urge to take revenge. In their anger, human beings used to justify "the act of taking revenge", against wicked fellows. Human beings have a tendency to justify their wicked actions. Christians too have a tendency to justify killing of wicked people, or even of good people of other nations, tribes or family members.

Christians should agree that God would never allow killing of any kind of people by Christians, or even by non Christians. It is out of their own choice and out of their freedom that they used to kill each other, as a fulfillment of their own emotional irritation. Moses was no exceptional. Christians should never justify killing of any kind, only because Moses, a man used by God, also killed an Egyptian. Killing remained a dark spot in the life of Moses. Although, God forgave his past killing, killing cannot be an imitable action for Christians.

3

Israelites' War With Enemies Do not have any Divine Permission

3.1. War with the Amalekites

After coming out of Egypt, the first war the Israelites fought, was that war with the Amalekites before entering Canaan (Exodus 17:8-16). According to this passage, in Exodus, the Israelites used to win as long as Moses could stretch out or lift up his hands (or arms). What kind of hands (or arms) had Moses that through its stretching out, or lifting of it, that Israelites could win war (or battle) against Amalekites? Or what power was there in his hands? It is possibly true to say that, God really gave power to the hands of Moses to achieve mission of love to the gentile nations. However, since Moses was not like Jesus, he could have forgotten the purpose of the power given to him. Instead of using the power given to him to achieve a mission of love to the gentile nations, he used it to fight against the gentiles. If this view is true, it must meant that he misused it as he was unable to distinguish his own Israelite will from that of God. He was not supposed to use the power given to him for fighting war. But since he confused his own will to be the will of God, he wrongly used the power given to him.

Jesus was able to differentiate his own will from the will of God. The same power given to Moses was given to him too. His own desire tempted him to use the power given to him for his own satisfaction. His own desire tempted him to use this power to turn stones into bread. It was a strong temptation as he was hungry for forty days. To human beings it is nothing wrong to use divine power given to use it to turn stones into bread and eat of it. Moses too used the same or similar power given to him to fight with Amalekites. Any human being who would meet or face such a difficult situation, he/she would not open any chance to think twice than to say "What is wrong to use the power given to me to turn stones into bread and be happy." Moses too must have taken that way. He was given the same or at least a similar power to do good to his enemies, but he failed to realize this. Instead of being like Jesus, he misused the power given to him to fight the enemies. Because, of this Moses failed to be more like Jesus. In waging war with other nations, Moses failed in the temptation, as he used the power given to him to fulfill his own need or the need of Israel. If Moses would be reincarnated, or be born again, he may not fight again with other nations.

3.2. War with the Amorites

The second battle Israelites fought with was that with the Amorites on their way to Canaan. (Numbers 21:21-32). Israelites might claim that their war with Amorites that time was a punishment for their disobedience to their humble request to pass through their land. However, it is inferable to say that if they fore knew the non-violence of Jesus they must be patient enough to wait for some more days or weeks for their permission. If they would believe God to do miracles, they must also believe God to make Amorites become kindful enough to allow Israelites pass through their land. If Israelites were closer to God than were Amorites, they must use non-violence, even if Amorites tried to wage war against them. The God of love and the true God must not allow Israelites to wage war against Amorites. The real God and the God of all nations cannot agree with Israelites war with other nations.

3.3. War with Og King of Bashan

The third battle of Israelites fought with other nations in the Exodus might be that war/battle with Og, king of Bashan. Here too, there was no evidence for God's permission for Israelites' war/battle with Og, king of Bashan. With the mind of war/enmity, Israelites simply fought with Og, king of Bashan. Even if they did ask God, they would not be able to wait for God's answer. Even if they were able to wait for God's answer, God would told them to have peaceful solution of the problem with Og. God must wish Israelites to have the most peaceful solution to their problem with Og. War with Og, is the choice of Israelites rather than that of God.

3.4. War with the Medianites

Another battle of Israelites with enemies was with Medianites (Num. 31:1-12). According to the writer, the Lord asked Moses to punish the Medianites for their wickedness. Here, Moses was told that he would die after punishing the Medianites. Here too, it should not be taken as God's voice which told Moses to punish the Mideanites for their wickedness. Because, it is totally wrong to claim that the true God, the God of love, the Father and Mother of all, would ask wicked Israelites to punish wicked Medianites. Although, both groups are wicked, God would accept them as his wicked children. Since both groups are his children God would never allow war between them.

3.5. The Fall of Jericho

The fall of the city of Jericho (Joshua 6:1-27) was another case of Israelites' war with other nations. The fall of Jericho was said to be the result of the Israelites compassing or going round the city once everyday. On the seventh day, they went around the city seven times, as a result of it, the city fell into the hands of the Israelites. To say that the city fell into the hands of the Israelites is different from saying that the walls of the city of Jericho fell into the ground." The wall fell down flat" means the second sense. The former view "that the city fell into the hands of the Israelites" does not necessarily involved miracle. The second view "that the walls of the city fell flat," sounds to involve miracle, if it is taken as a result only of shouting and going round the city within seven days. However, miracles may be excluded even if the walls of the city fell as a result of the marching around of the city……Even if one takes the involvement of miracle in the fall, it may be taken as a result of the faith and earnestness of the Israelites but not as a result of God's involvement in punishing the people of Jericho. Israel might gain profit from the fall of Jericho. However, the fall of Jericho has nothing to do with the extension of the Kingdom of God. If God would have the right to intervene in the conflict between Israelites and the people of Jericho, he must have protected Jericho from the hands of the Israelites. However, at the creation, God is believed to limit himself to the extent that he (God) cannot interfere himself with human actions, because he made them free. Accordingly, God did not interfere with the actions of Israel in their war with Gentiles.

The miraculous work in the fall of Jericho is resulted by the faith of Israel, and should not be taken as the work of God. God cannot interfere with the wicked actions of human beings. He cannot be taken as involving himself in the wicked actions of Israelites against their enemies. The enemies of Israel could never be the enemies of the true God. This belief must have been only a presumption of Israelite leaders. This view could even be hated by God, instead accepting it.

3.6. War with the City of AI

The next battle Israelites fought was that with the city of Ai (Joshua 8:1-29). This battle must be misinterpreted in the following ways. (1) It might not be the real God who asked Joshua and the Israelites to attack and take the city of Ai. It must really be the God in the mind and wish of the Israelites who would have asked Joshua and the Israelites to attack the city of Ai. The just God and Father/Mother of all cannot have supported Israelites in their fight against other nations. This cannot be denied. However, the Israelites must have favoured themselves only to destroy other children of God. It might only be an idol who could be thought to destroy people of Ai in favour of the Israelites. If a God could do that he must be lesser than God.

(2) Israelites' view of God's actions against people of Ai in favour of people of Israel must have been based not on facts or truths, but rather on the wrong notion of Israel as the chosen nation, the holy nation, from among all the nations of the world. Israel as a nation felt that they are the chosen nation, and that other nations are enemies of God. Israel, therefore, would think that God fought for Israel.

These points are some of the reasons why Israelites thought that God fought for Israel against other nations.

3.7. War with Amorites

Israelites fought also with the five kings of the Amorites (Joshua 10:1-15). The five kings of Amorites were- the king of Jerusalem, the king of Hebron, the king of Jasmuth, the king of Lachish, and the the king of Eglon. The following corrections for the passage need to be done in order to know the truth.

(a) In verse 8, the writer must have put human (his own) words into the mouth of God. Because God (Yahweh) is the God of both Amorites and Israelites and Parent of both nations. It must be the writer's composition for the Lord.

(b) The sentence "And the Lord threw them into panic before Israel..." in verse 10 is not a right interpretation of the facts. The right interpretation must be that " when they were defeated by the Israelites they were filled with panic. If some one could read the mind of God at that moment he must felt pity with the Amorites, as they were defeated by the Israelites.

(c) "The Lord threw down huge stones from heaven on them..." in verse 11 should be a wrong interpretation of the Israelites. The right way of writing must be "The defeat of the Amorites in the hands of the Israelites was coincided with the down pouring of hailstones which killed more people than those killed by Israelites".

(d) In verse 12, the phrase "On the day when the Lord gave the Amorites over to the Israelites Joshua spoke to the Lord...?" should be corrected as follows: "On the day when the Israelites overcame/defeated Amorites, Joshua spoke (as if) to the Lord...".

(e) The words of Joshua, "Sun, stand still at Gibeon, and Moon, in the valley of Aijalon," implies the following: (i) In ancient times, the world understood the Sun as moving around the earth, in the same way as the Moon moves around the earth. (ii). Since God is Parent of both groups He would not try to side with the Israelites against other nations. Therefore it is not necessary for God to stop the Sun and the Moon to make a day longer. God need not help Israelites committing

> the sin of war. God has no need to make Israelites success in their wicked campaign against their neighbours. (iii) It is not even needed to make the day longer, only to make Israelites successful in their wicked campaign against other children of God. God would not involve himself in Joshua's wish to stop the Sun for some reasons. (i) God who is all-knowing would not even suggested to stop the Sun and the Moon, because the situation was the situation of God's children warring with other children of God. God should not and did not involve himself in Israelites' war against Amorites, both of whom were God's children. God did not like to do something against his children Amorites in favour of his children Israelites. (ii) But it is not even necessary to make that day longer.

So, we can say that what is wrong in the passage is one of the following:

(i) It might be Joshua's ignorance which caused him to say the unnecessary saying, Sun, stand still at Gibeon, and Moon, in the valley of Aijalon" If Joshua knew the truth about the Sun, he would never say that. If it was not the mistake of Joshua, then he should say what caused him putting that way.

Whatever it be, what we want to say is that God did not involve himself in the mistake of the saying that the Sun and the moon could be stopped. The situation did not even necessitate the claim made.

3.8. The Defeat of United Kings of Canaan

Here, too, Israelite leaders' thought that the Lord ordered Israelites to fight the united kings of Northern Canaan. In reality the LORD is God both of the Israelites and that of the united kings. Therefore, it is wrong to think that the God and Father/Mother of all could allow Israelites to wage war with other nations. The phrase "The LORD said to Joshua" is a wrong addition to the history of Israel. God is the leader of Israel as long as they do his will. However, they should not try to use God as they used their spears, and swords. It was not God who fought war with them. Rather it was Israelites who thought that God fought with them. How can they use God as they used their bow and arrow in wars?

It is true to say that Israelites often won wars whenever they had better war strategy, better and stronger army, or even when they have better knowledge of the place they were fighting with enemies. It is a sin for them to claim that God supported their sins against enemies. This means that when Israelites claimed that God supported their wars against enemies, it also means that God sinned with Israelites. God must not agree with this.

These are few cases of Israelites' war with other nations which developed the religious history of the Israelites. We may now discuss the reasons for Israel's failure to live according to the will of God.

(1) The greatest mistake of the Israelites was their view that God is the God of Israel alone. He is the God of all human beings all the time. Even when other nations do not know him, he is their God. All worship God without proper knowledge about him. Israelites did not know this..

(2) Basing on this they understood God, who is Father and Mother of all nations. Although, God is Father and Mother of all nations, Israelites wrongly understood him to be their own Father only. They did not know the truth that God is the God of all nations.

(3) They thought that killing in war is not a sin. Although, they are told that murder is sin, they wrongly thought that killing in war is nothing wrong. Due to this wrong knowledge of the truth, they regarded war as a part of true human life.

(4) They wrongly regarded people of other nations as enemies of Israelites, and enemies of God as well. Due to this and other reasons, Israelites regarded waging war as a part of their life. They even have the idea of Holy War. War is an evil which can never be holy. There can be holy war only if war is the will of God. But war is an evil in the sight of God. Those who fought war are sinners.

4

Judges' War With Other Nations Have no Divine Permission

This chapter is particularly for Israelites' war with other nations under the leadership of the judges of Israel. Judges were no different from earlier leaders like Moses, Joshua, Caleb and others. They did not have any negative attitude to war. They did not even claim that they fought war with other nations only because the situation necessitate war. They even claimed that God took the initiative part in most of the wars they fought. A brief looked at some of the wars fought under the leadership of the Judges may be done below.

4.1. Othniel and Ehud

Othniel seemed to be the first judge who fought with other nations. During his time no Israelite was so close to God to realize the evil of war. Othniel fought war with king Cushan-Rishathaim of Aram. He was ignorant of the evil of war. Even the writer was ignorant of God's will about war. The writer says," the Lord gave king Cu'shan-Rish-a-tha-im of Aram into his hands..." (Jud. 3:10). It is not what God did. It was the writer's own interpretation of history. While God hated war, the writer claimed that God involved himself in Israelites' war against enemies.

During the time of Ehud too, Israelites fought war with other nations. According to them they were defeated in war by king Eglon of Moab, because of their sins. This too was a wrong interpretation of history. Amorites and Amalekites defeated Israelites during the time of Ehud, only because enemies have stronger army than that of Israel, but not because God left them alone. Israelites served king Eglon of Moab for eighteen years only because Eglon had a more powerful army than that of Israelites.

When Ehud became a judge, he committed the sin of killing Eglon. He was an enemy of the teaching of Jesus who says "do not resist an evil doer. But if anyone strikes you on the right cheek, turn the other also..." (Matt. 5:39). "Love your enemies... (Matt. 5:43) .etc.... Ehud committed two sins together on the day he killed Eglon. In order to make the way to commit the sin of killing Eglon, Ehud first committed the sin of cheating him (Judges 3:20-23). Ehud told lie when he says, "Follow me, for the Lord has given your enemies the Maobites into your hands". (3:28). God did not involve himself in wars. It was Israelites themselves who wrongly claimed God to involve himself in their wars.

4.2. Deborah and Barak

Deborah and Barak were too weak. They did not know what the will of God is and what is not. They did not have any other solution to the problem of the Israelites. Instead of seeking peaceful solution to the problem in relation to their neighbours, Deborah and Barak too fought war against other nations as a means to solve their problem.

Deborah told lie when she says to Barak, "The Lord, the God of Israel, commands you, Go take position at mount Tabor, bring ten thousand from ... Zebulun..." (Judge. 4:6). This is a case of human words put into the mouth of God. It is unthinkable that God would suggest anything for Israelites' war with other nations, as much as it was unthinkable for the father of the prodigal son to ask the elder brother to fight with the younger brother.

4.3. Gideon

Gideon was a man of God. He was a faithful servant of God. He was lover of his people. His quality as a leader is that he loved Israelites as a nation. He felt sad for the political inability of his people. However, he was not able to discover the sinfulness of war or killing in war. He positively fought war as if it was the will of God. Although, he was a man of God he did not know that he committed sin in waging war against other children of God. Gideon was not a perfect man. So, his act of waging war was a black spot in his life. No one should justify war only because a man of God like him waged war. Although, Gideon was a man of God, his life was not a perfect example for Christian life. The bright side of his life may be an example for Christian life; however bad examples in his life should not be taken as an example for Christian life.

If Gideon was meek as a man of God and have better leadership quality, he must have better and peaceful solution with the wrong attitude of people of Succoth (cf. Jug. 8: 5-6). Verses 7 & 9 showed the immaturity and revengeful nature of Gideon.

As a whole we would say that Gideon's involvement in wars with other nations is the dark spot in his life. One cannot take war as good only because Gideon involved himself in wars. Since war is an evil, his involvement in wars made his life partly darkened?

4.4. Abimelech

Abimelech too followed the footsteps of his predecessors in waging war against their neighbouring nations. The (or a) writer of Judges made a wrong statement when he says that it was God who caused enmity between Abimelech and the lords of Sechem. Israelites misunderstood God merely as an evil spirit who would cause enmity between it and other nations. God should be pictured at least more than evil spirits. He should be more like a peace maker than one who cause enmity between nations. It was not God who caused lords of Sechem to hate Abimelech. It must be due to the wickedness of lords of Sechem, that there was war between them and Abimelech. One should not think that he/she can use God as he/she used his/her dao, or other instruments. God should be left to follow his own principles of working. We should not try to force him do our own works. It is not God's duty to join Israelites in their war with other nations.

4.5. Samson

Samson did not have any negative attitude to war. He accepted war as his duty as if it is a traditional culture of human beings. He waged war with the Philistines, to which his wife Delilah belonged. Samson waged war, not because it was the will of God, but only

(a) he thought that it was the will of God,
(b) because he thought that it is a necessary means to punish enemies of God;
(c) that even his predecessors too fought wars, and that his duty is to successfully wage war;
(d) he thought that killing in war is not a sin.
Therefore, war cannot be taken as acceptable attitude to others only because Samson too fought war with other nations.

As a whole Israelites fought war with other nations under the leadership of the judges too as they thought that God not only allow them to do so, but even order them to fight war with them, and that he used to lead them in wars as captain of the army of Israel. Moreover, they used to talk of presence of holy wars. Still another reason for them to continue wars under the leadership the judges is that judges were not able to discover the sinfulness of war with other nations or other children of God. No nation should imitate their warring attitude to other nations.

5

Kings' War With Other Nations Do not Prove Divine Permission for War

Since ancient Israelites believed that killing in war is not sin, and that even God used to initiate Israelites' war with other nations, no ancient Israelite king was free from waging war. The first king, Saul, not only regarded waging war as a necessary means to have national security, but even regarded it as the will of God. David, Solomon and Rehoboam were no different from him. Kings in the divided Kingdoms, too followed the footsteps of their predecessors in case of war. They did not know any right solution to inter national problems or conflicts. They might think that "War alone is the only solution to such issues." We shall have the possible study of each of them.

5.1. Saul's War With Other Nations

When Israelites asked Samuel to appoint a king for them, Israelites put their words into the mouth of God, as follow; "... for they have not rejected you, but they have rejected me from being king over them." (I Sam. 8:7). When Israelites saw other nations having kings to lead them in wars, they too wanted to have kings to lead them in wars. However, according to most religious view of the time, their request for king showed that they no more trust God to be their leader in wars. Another meaning of this is that they wanted to have kings to lead them in wars, by rejecting the will of God which is peaceful co-existence with other nations. Looking at the statement quoted above from the perspective of the teachings of Jesus, the rejection of God is in that they chose to have kings against a non-violent means of God.

Saul was chosen to fulfill the request of the people, because even God could not do anything to them against their wish. The first war Saul fought with after he became king was that with the Amorites. (I Samuel 11:1-15). In this war the writer's interpretation of what had happened, "Then the dread of the Lord fell upon the people and they came out as one". (I Sam. 11:7), should be corrected by one or both of the followings:

(a) "Then the dread of the Lord fell upon the people because they wrongly regarded the order as if it came from God."
(b) Then the dread of Saul and Samuel fell upon the people and they came out as one." Both or one of them must be taken as true.

The next battle Saul fought with was that with Philistines (I Sa. 14:1-35). Here some verses need to be corrected. "So, the Lord gave Israel the victory that day", (I Sam. 14:23 a) should be re-written as, "So, Israel had victory that day" This is true because

(a) God never involved himself in Israelites' war against others.
(b) For God other nations too were his beloved children as much as Israelites were. God would not side with Israelites against them. So, we can say, it was not God who gave victory to Israelites over other nations.

Another war fought by Saul was that with Amalekites (I Sam. 15:1-9). The words of the Israelites which they put into the mouth of God, recorded in 15:2", I will punish the Amalekites for what they did to opposing the Israelites when they came out of Egypt…"), should be corrected as follow: "King Saul and the Israelites will punish the Amalikites for what they did in opposing the Israelites when they came out of Egypt. "Saul was as sinful as the Amalekites were. Therefore, it is wrong to say that God punished the Amalekites through the Israelites.

5.2. David's War with Other Nations

David also fought war. He was a good king for some reasons. But he was not a perfect king. His weakness cannot be a part of the truth. His weaknesses must be taken as the dark spots in his life. His love for war must be taken as the dark spot in his life.

David fought war when he tried to avenge the destruction of Ziklag. (I Sam. 30:1-31). It is totally wrong to say that God said to David, "Go up, for I will certainly give the Philistines into your hand." (2 Sam. 5:19). How could the Father and Mother of all human beings handed over the Philistines into the hands of the Israelites only to be destroyed by Israelites? It is only the wish and view of Israelites that God did it that way. "God is not the spear and sword of the Israelites. "Let God be God." Let not God be the dao of the Israelites. God cannot be the robot and puppet of the Israelites. God is more, not only than robots and puppets, but also than human beings.

The sentence, "David also struck down King Hada. de'zerson of Rehob of Zo'bbah", (Sam. 8:3) shows

(1) That the mind of David is completely the opposite of the mind of God. (2) That he had no mercy on the victimized people (3) instead he victimized any possible opponent (4) he had no idea at all that his enemies too would be children of God. (5) It even seemed to show that there is no deep knowledge of God in David's life, etc. (6) that he wanted to live at the expenses of the life of his neighbours. (7) That David did not even realize the value of living peacefully (together) with his neighbours. (8) that he is a selfish creature who want to live alone on earth or at least wanted to live on earth as a hero over others. Another sentence "… David killed twenty thousand men of the Arameans" shows (1) That he had no mercy, no compassion, no love in him. (2) David could be only a man who loved only those who love him. The sentence "The Lord gave victory to David wherever he went", (2 Sam. 8: 6; 8:14), is not based on God's actions or doings, but on the wish, concepts and beliefs of the Israelites. The sentence is not based on facts, but on wrong views about God. It is not based on what God did, but on what Israelites wished him. God may be angry upon the writer and the standard of Israelites. It is very funny to see Israelites saying that God gave victory

to one of his children over against his other children. According to a sentence in 2 Samuel 8:13, David won a name for the poor and the victimized, but for killing so many victimized or vulranables. David also killed seven hundred chariot team and forty thousand horsemen (2 Sam. 11:18). One of the darkest spots in the life of David would be his act of killing Uriah as a step to get his wife Bathsheba (2 Sam. 10:14-26).

There is no part in David's life to condemn war and killing. David was too weak to realize the fact that war or any killing is sin against God. Since David was weak, his involvement in killing of any kind or killing in war cannot justify war and killing. His involvement in war should be taken as his sin against God. Because, God never allows war. Claims for God's permission for war in David's life are Israelite claims based on their own situation, against the will of God.

5.3. Solomon's War with Other Nations

Solomon did not have the extraordinary wisdom and knowledge of God which would help him discover the truth that war is evil, or sin. Although, Solomon fought lesser wars with other nations he did not develop any idea against war. But this does not prove that war is true.

Almost all the kings of ancient Israel and Judah fought wars against other nations. They all took positive stand in case of wars. However, a general study of the history of Israel only shows that Israelites had the following wrong claims:

(a) That they alone are God's people and other nations are God's enemies. So, God fought for them. God is warrior, captain of the army, etc.
(b) That although murder is sin (Exo. 20:13), killing in war is not sin, and is God's punishment for sins of sinners.
(c) In killing enemies in war they (Israelites) are instrumental for God's punishment of sinners. God used them in war to punish wicked nations.

(d) Not only that, there are holy wars too. God initiated those holy wars and used to play a great role in the victories against nations.
(e) So, they used to claim that God used to speak verbally to them giving them permission to wage wars against nations.

However, the truth appeared to be the opposite. We need to trust the following evaluation as true to correct the Jewish mistake in the Bible.

(a) That the idea of election of Israel plays no important role in God's economy of salvation. God's acceptance of human beings is based on faith.
(b) Even if Israel is chosen it (Israel) is chosen to spread the good news to other nations, rather than to take other nations as enemies.
(c) That God is mother–father of all human beings and all human beings are children of God. And that Israel is no better nation than other nations. Why should God punish other nations through Israel in wars?
(d) That killing of human kinds of any kind is sin against God. Exodus 20:13 should be taken to refer to all kinds of killing.
(e) Since killing of all kinds is sin, there is no holy war. Holy war should be there only in the mind of the wicked.
(f) God might have finished a great laughter on hearing the Israelites portraying him as warrior, captain of the army, etc.
(g) Truth should always be the same. The life of Jesus shows us the fact that non-violence is the eternal truth which is to be taken normative to judge war and peace in the Old Testament too.

6

Holy Wars

Ancient Israelites claimed to have holy wars. They regarded war with other nations as holy for certain reasons. 1. Israelites described Yahweh as a warrior (the Lord of hosts), who made Israel his people by the overthrow of the Egyptians (Exo. 15:1-18, Deut. 4:34). Yahweh maintains Israel as such by fighting (I Sam. 22:35; Ps. 144:1). According to Exodus 12:41, Israel as an army, is the hosts of Yahweh. The victories of Israel are all ascribed to Yahweh, and enemies of Israel and the enemies of Yahweh are one and the same.[1] (Judge 5; cf.) The Book of the Wars of the Lord. (Num. 21:14). Since Israel is an elected nation, all her enemies are the enemies of Yahweh, so all nations are the enemies of God. Golfwalt is quoted to say that the "Holy War" in David's time and earlier was the voluntary collaboration of tribes related to one another in religious covenant to gain and defend "the living space of an egalitarian independence movement."[2] Although, the practice of "holy war" partly changed, the idea of "holy war" had far reaching effects on later Judaism. The view of God as "The Divine Warrior" (cf. Ps. 24/23/:8) was later expressed further by the designation "Yahweh of hosts". Accordingly Yahweh was the commander of all Supernatural power as well as the armies of Israel.[3] The Exodus was regarded as a symbol of Yahweh's glorious victory over the Egyptians.[4] In this song of Moses the phrase "The Lord is a man of war," expresses the belief that he fought for Israel. Moses believed that it was Yahweh who cast Pharaoh's chariots and his army into the sea. It is the right-hand of the Lord which clashed the enemy in pieces. Moses thought that enemies those who rose against Israel rose against God himself. The wrath of the Lord had consumed the enemies like stubble. A note of ***henotheism*** too appeared in this song. Yahweh is glorified over other gods. Yahweh is more than other gods, because he overcame them in wars. The Psalms used the same language about the exodus and the occupation of Canaan.[5] Holy War" was originally conceived as Yahweh's battle on behalf of his people. Prophetic belief on holy war often turns to be more spiritual than physical. Prophets often predicted the fall of Israel, instead of fighting for Israel. It is our wonder how ancient Israelites who claimed themselves to be very spiritual, could wrongly understood God to be a great warrior, captain of the army of Israel, the Lord of hosts, the one who ordered Israelites to fight enemies.

However, we, as Christians, are able to realize the fact that every theological concept has some changes or developments throughout human history. According to this, concepts, ideologies, theological views underwent some changes from time to time, through which some wrong ones used to be discarded, while true and new ideas, concepts used to replace them. In other words, the history of Israel shows that some wrong concepts or theological views during the time of Moses could be corrected in the time of the 'Jewish prophets. Accordingly, Israelites' attitude to war too has undergone remarkable changes. During the intertestamental period, more emphasis is made on warfare against ungodly might, and against sin (Eth. Enoch 94). In the New Testament we saw a kind of non-resistance, which became the opposite of ancient Israelites' view of God involving himself in war against other nations. The N.T. study would show us that the people of God are not only to follow the law of non-violence, but even to love one's enemies, and even feed one's hungry and thirsty enemy.

Endnotes

1. Cf. Alan Richardson, (edt.*), A Theological Word Book of the Bible,* London, 1988, p. 278.
2. Quoted by C. Colin, "War" in *The New Int. Dictionary of NT Theology,* Cumbria, 1986, p. 960. quoted from N.K. Gottwald, "War, Holy", *IDB Supplementary Volume,* 1976, p. 942.
3. Cf. *Ibid.*

4. Cf. Ps. 15:1 – 2.
5. Psalms 132; 131:12, 16, 18.
   Cf. Amos 2:6-14; Ezekiel 5; Isaiah 40:2.

7

Consultation of Prophets and God

There are certain cases in the Old Testament of Israelites consulting prophets and God in many occasions for war with other nations. One example is in I Samuel 30:7-8. Here in this passage David consulted God, not only in an ordinary way. He used the ephod of priest Abiathar, son of Abime-e-lech, and consulted the Lord, whether the Lord would allow him to deliver his people from the hands of the Amalekites. Amalekites had smitten the city of Ziklag and took away the wives and children of David and his army men. Instead of immediately running after the Amalekites David consulted God, as to whether he would chase them or not. God was said to allow them to deliver their people. God was said to answer that David and his people must overtake Amalekites and recover their wives and children. Nothing was said whether God agreed with David's use of the Priest's (Abiathar's) ephod to consult God for the war.

It is true to say that Israelites used to consult God through the ephod of the priest. Anyone or individual could use anything to consult God. However, it is totally another case as to whether God would accept these mediums of consultation or not. The question of whether God would ever accept this medium or not is the same question as to whether worship of God in a particular place either at Jerusalem or at mount Gerazim is a possible worship of God.

It is not fully true to say that Jesus totally rejected worship at mount Zion in Jerusalem and worship at Mount Gerazim. (John

4:21-24). It should be said that although God would accept all kinds of worship as worship, he is supposed not to accept the wrong means of worship. God must have (partially) accepted Israelites 'worship of God at Mount Zion alone, and Samaritans' worship at Mount Gerazim. However, Jesus shows us the fact that he (God) did not accept particularization of places of worship. Because, as much as God has a reigning power everywhere, he could be worshipped everywhere. What we can say here is that God accepts every worship of him. It must be said that although God did not accept particularization of worship at such temples, he partially accepted any worship in general. In other words, God accepts worship of him by Israelites and Samaritans on the basis of their attitudes to him, but not on the basis of places of worship. So, Jesus did not totally rejected worship of God by Israelites. He rejected only the way of worship, i.e., worship of God only at mount Zion and at mount Gerezim.

In the same way, consultation of God is a right attitude of worship. However, consultation of God by means of the ephod of the priest too is a particularization of such consultation. It cancels the faith and meekness of the one who consulted God. If Jesus' partial condemnation of worship at Jerusalem temple and at Mount Gerazim be true, then he is liable to condemn Israelites' consultation of God through the ephod of the priest. Particularization or concentration of worship at a particular place is wrong as much as used of the ephod of the priest for consultation was wrong.

Not only was the means wrong or weak, but the subject of consultation too was wrong. For David, it was right to bring back his people. However, war or violence was not the right means to bring them back. To use war as a means to bring them back is to use the means and ways of heathens but not of God's people. If David was a real man of God, he must have chosen the best ways and means to bring them back. If he used war to do something important, he had an early disobedience to Paul when Paul says, "Do not be conformed to this world….." (Romans 12:1-2). David was only imitating a way of life of the would be heathen people when he chose war or violence as a means to bring back his people. It must not be God who responded positively to David's consultation. It must be something else which responded positively to David. It would have been David's view which positively responded to him. David's use of violence or war should not be taken as an example for God's people to be imitated.

Another case of Israelite kings asking the prophets and God whether they would fight with enemies or whether He (God) would go with them in the war, is I Kings 22: The prophets' answer is that Ahab and Jehoshaphat could fight the city of Ramoth-gil-e-ad and would defeat them. Prophets numbering four hundred claimed that the Lord would help them triumph over enemies. While other prophets promised that God would help Ahab and Jehoshaphat in their war with Ramoth-gil-e-ad in Syria, prophet Micaiah did not hide the truth that God would not fight for Israel and Judah. (I Kg. 22:17-28). All the four hundred prophets (probably false prophets) told the two kings that God would go with them in their fight against the city of Ramoth-gil-e-ad. Without knowing the will of God, these prophets told the two kings according to the traditional belief of the Israelites that God used to fight for Israel. It is also in their intention to please the two kings that they told the two that way.

Prophet Micaiah must be taken as true prophet who was not afraid to tell the truth about the stand of God, which may be against the wish of the two kings. Although, he knew that the two kings would be angry upon him for saying that God would not go with them to fight with their enemies, he, with fear or without fear, told the truth that God would not go with them to fight with the enemies. This truth should be expanded by us even to put the words of Micaiah as, God should/would/will never fight for Israel/Judah against their enemies. Prophet Micaiah alone seems to be the only prophet who knew the will of the Lord, and proclaim the truth that God would never allow war between nations. Micaiah's stand may also be taken to claim that it is not only at this time, but that God hates war forever. This passage can be taken to show that claims for God to support Israelites' war with other nations must be the claim of false prophets and the people of Israel.

Our study shows that although Israelites in ancient time used to ask God as to whether he (God) would fight for them in their fight against enemies, the answer used to be their own made answers, rather than God's real answer. Therefore, we cannot accept the claim that God promised Israelites to go for war as he (God) has to fight for Israel.

8

The View That God Punishes Nations by Means of Wars

The view that God punishes nations through or by means of war was an accepted view among ancient Israelites. When a nation is defeated in war it used to be taken as God's punishment as a result of their sinfulness. For example when Amalekites were defeated in war, it was taken to be their punishment as a result of their sins against God. When the city of Jericho was taken by Israelites, Jericho fell into the hands of the Israelites because they (people of Jericho) were sinners as a result of which they became enemies of God too. However, when Israelites were being defeated in war, it used to be because of their sins. Israelites too were punished due to their sins. It was thought to be because of the sin against God that Israelites were once defeated in war by the people of Ai. Israelites claimed that sin is the cause of their defeat in that battle. Although, they tried to spiritualize war, it is wrong to do so. The main reason for their defeat is that the enemy had better and stronger army, and the enemy had more number of people to fight in that war. Since God never fight for the Israelites, victory in war depended on better army, better army strategy, stronger army, better knowledge of the battle field, etc. God has nothing to do with war.

When the city of Ai fell into the hands of the Israelites, Israelites would think that God gave victory to Israelites because they are the chosen people of God and that Ai fell into their hands because of their (the people of Ai) sins against God. Due to this concept in mind, Israelites often take into granted that gentile nations often fell into their hands due to their (other nations) sins.

In around 721/722 B.C. the Northern Kingdom of Samaria was invaded by Shalmanesser, king of Assyria. He took Samaria and deported its people to Assyria, as captives.[6] This was taken as a result of their sins against God.[7] Israelites were not always good to God. However, as long as they gained victory in wars, they would think that they are the holy nation. However, when they would be defeated in war as such, and be deported to other countries, they would say that it is because of their immeasurable sins.

In the same way when the Jews were invaded in 597 and 587 BC by the Babylonians under king Nebuchadnezzar of Babylon, Jerusalem fell into their hands. At that time Jedekiah was king of the Southern Kingdom of Judah. At that time the Babylonians took Jerusalem and deported so many Jews to Babylon. To a Jew it was God's punishment of the Jews due to their stubbornness against him. Moreover, some of them would even take the view either that Yahweh had abandoned his people, or that the popularity, nationality or even culture of the Jews were eliminated due to their sins. Minor sins cannot cause this. Their sins which could cause this kind of deportation which became a captivity to other nations must be grave sins which could not be forgiven or forgotten so easily. Moreover, the destruction of the temple at Jerusalem would be taken (a) that Yahweh is no more superior to the gods of other nations (b) or that Jews were no more his people, that he abandoned them to become captives to other nations. (c) that they became no people, no nation, etc. (d) Other nations now could think that the God of Israel/Jews, is either (i) weaker than the gods of other nations or (ii) That he is not true God, and as such he could not protect the Jews.

The view that God punishes wicked nations by means of defeat in war is wrong for certain reasons. (a) God never immediately punishes any one due to his/her/their sins. He must punish sinners one day, probably only at the last judgment. So, it is wrong to claim that God punishes wicked nations by means of defeat in war against enemies.

(b) God is a patient or long-suffering God. He is patient enough to await for the sinner's repentance. So, it is wrong to claim that God used wars to punish wicked nations. (c) God is not a violent God. He cannot use war like wicked kings to punish wicked nations. He should not be pictured as wicked kings who would punish disobedient and rebellious nations. (d) God is the Good God, and so he cannot use wicked means to deal with his wicked children, immediately. Since God is good, he use forgiveness to deal with sinners. God's responsibility is to wait for the repentance of sinners so that they may be forgiven of their sins. (e) Since all human beings are God's children, he (God) cannot use one nation to punish other nations, as much as he cannot use one son to kill his other son. (f) Generally, war is not God's means of punishing nations. (g) Israelites, in reality, were no better nation than other nations. God cannot especially love a particular nation. (h) We cannot make God in our own images. God should be pictured as he is, but not as we are.

Endnotes

6. 2 Kings 17:5.
7. Cf. 2 Kings 17:7.

9

Human Beings Made God in their Own Images

To say that God is a warrior is one case of human beings made God in their own images. To say that God is a warrior is no less a mistake than to say that God is a drunkard. As much as it is wrong to say that "God is a drunkard", it is also wrong to say that God is a warrior. We have a tendency to say that calling God a warrior is "making God in a human image". The same is with calling God as "Captain of the army". In the Old Testament the title "Captain of the army" is a favorite title for God, because he is believed to lead the Israelite army in the battle field as its captain. To call God "Captain of the army" means, to me, to regard God as a sinner. Because, to me, war is an evil, those who fought war are evil human beings. In that sense, if God be made "Captain of the army" it is making God a sinner, unless this "army" is taken to refer to spiritual army. To call God "Captain of the army" is to make God in human image.

When Israelites used to claim that God permitted them to go to war against their enemies, this too has the same implication. To claim that God permitted Israelites to go to war against other nations, is a little better than to call him "Captain of the army" who fought for Israel against other nations, as its leader in war. The title "warrior" is one who fought most, not necessarily as its leader, but as one of those who fought war. On the other hand "One who permitted Israelites to go to war against other nations" could be a lesser god who sided with one nation against other nations.

Other ways of describing the same thing is to say that "God fought for and with Israel against other nations". These two phrases could be used to describe the first two titles such as God as "warrior" and "Captain of the army". To say that God went to the battle field "to fight for Israel " is only making the same thing stated in a longer sentence. To describe God as such is only to draw the picture of God in human forms. To describe God as "warrior", "Captain of the army", "permitting Israelites to fight with other nations", is to describe God in our human images. In order to understand what we meant by saying 'human beings made God in their own images", let us learn some more imageries used in the Old Testament to describe God.

A writer of Genesis[8] claimed that after the flood (of Noah) was subsided, Noah offered a sacrifice, and as soon as the odour of the sacrifice reached God, he was so happy that he changed his attitude to sinful human beings. Here God is pictured as man/woman who love to eat meat so much. It is possible for meat loving human beings to be pleased so much when they smelt the odour of meat curries. Here God is pictured as human being who love to eat meat. It is one case of making God in our own images.

Writers of the Old Testament often described God in human imageries. God talked with Adam and Eve. They have heard the footsteps of God. God could hear human voices. God can see, hear, talk, smell, and so on. God is also described as one who took revenges. He is an angry God, he is wrathful, God.

It is not totally wrong to describe God in human imageries. Human beings could describe God only in human imageries. Because, human reasoning, without deeper devotion to God, cannot comprehend God as he really is. Because, God is invisible, and so human beings cannot easily concentrate on unseen things. When they think of God only visible things on earth tends to come to their minds. In other words, they have a tendency to think of every metaphysical things from the standpoint of visible things. Therefore, they can hardly go beyond human imageries even to describe God. Moreover, since they used only human languages to describe God, their descriptions tend to make God human. Moreover, probably, it is true to say that God is personal, and has human qualities too. If so, it must be an unavoidable way to describe God as human being. However, in doing so, human beings could be right and wrong. Someone could rightly describe God as-Father and Mother or Parent. God could rightly be described as Lord, Creator, Saviour, etc.

However, we must be wrong to describe God from the perspective of sinful human situations. It is wrong to call God drunkard, smoker, adulterer, "warrior", captain of the army", join hands with Israelites to destroy enemies, fighting for Israel, etc. It may not be too wrong to say that in describing God that way, those who are closer to God through deeper faith may describe him more truly than those who are a little far away from God.

Although, it is true to describe God in human images, it is wrong to describe God from the perspective of sinful situations.

Endnotes

8. Genesis 8:20-22.

PART-2

NEGATIVE BIBLICAL VIEWS TO WAR/KILLING/VIOLENCE

There are a number of passages in the Bible which could be used to condemn killing of any kind, violence and war of any kind. Particular passages are chosen to prove that God must be against violence of any kind. According to the chosen passages we have enough points to condemn violence, killing of all kinds, war of all kinds. As far as possible such passages must be studied in detail.

10

Negative Attitude to War/Killing in the Pentateuch

Few passages are enough to prove that writers of the Pentateuch condemned killing or war as a sin.

10.1. Negative Attitude to Cain's killing of Abel

A writer of Genesis put a note of cursing in the mouth of God, which can be taken to condemn killing. According to this the earth became accursed because of the blood of Abel. As soon as Cain killed his brother Abel, the earth is accursed for which even the fertility of the soil is lost. In one sense, it is unthinkable to say that the blood of a person killed can simply made the earth barren. So, the passage must be taken in another sense. Since, the passage seemed to be a myth it should be taken as conveying spiritual message. Since killing of a person or a brother is a grave sin, such a sinful act caused accurse to the earth. However, today the situation is changing. Some tribals used to say that today killing of a man/woman is like killing a cock/hen. It means that killers no more hesitated to kill human beings as if they no more take the act as a sinful act. It also means that the number of killing is so much that it is almost equal to killing of cocks/hens.

However, it is quite imaginable to us to say that those who witnessed the first killing of human beings must have taken killing of human beings as the gravest sin. At such a situation it must be imaginable to say that the earth is accursed as soon as the blood of the first ever killed man dropped on the ground. It emphasized the fact of the gravity of the sin of killing a human being. The writer's word, "...the earth, which has opened its mouth to receive your brother's blood", too emphasizes the gravity of the sin of killing human beings. The passage is one of the best passages in the Bible to point out the sinfulness of killing human beings. It is true to everyone that because of human sinfulness the earth became accursed to reduce the earth as if it is equal to hell in the Jewish mind. Killing is the gravest sin which rendered the earth the uncomfortable place to live in. If there is no killing on earth it will remain a very comfortable place to live in. Sin made the earth very uncomfortable. The earth really is accursed due to human sinfulness, especially due to killing of human beings.

Ecologists would have interest in taking the passage to say that the earth is accursed as a result of human sinfulness against nature-against animals, against trees, against the atmosphere, against water, etc. Ecological crisis is the cursed state of the earth caused by human sinfulness. Human beings destroyed forests and killed animals so much so that ecological crisis has been caused. The earth becomes barren due to human sinfulness against trees and animals. The blood of human beings dropped on the ground symbolized human sinfulness affecting the earth.

Our study of Cain's killing of Abel shows us the fact that killing left the earth accursed. It is time for us to realize the fact that if there is no killing on earth it must still remain a comfortable place to live in.

10.2. The Sixth Commandment

You shall not kill
You shall not murder.

These two versions of the same verse or commandment made different senses. The first one "You shall not kill" can connote different meanings. (a) It can refer to killing/murdering of individuals. (b) It can also imply all kinds of killing of animals and human beings. If it be taken like this, killing of all kinds of animals must have been forbidden by the Israelite leaders. It can imply killing of both-killing of individuals (murder) and killing in war. So, "you shall not kill" can imply all these kinds of killings.

The second version "You shall not murder" must be a correction of the former translation according to Jewish understanding of it, to mean that the sixth law implies only killing of individual human beings. If so, it means to say "Do not kill individual human beings". This stand would be taken by some to say that for the Israelites, killing in war is permissible, because they have the belief that God often asks Israelites to fight in war against other nations. According to this Israelites used to go to war because they thought that God has permitted war and killing in war. Probably it is true to say that some versions of the Bible used "murder" here to denote that what is forbidden is only killing of individual human beings. So, it means that while killing in war is permitted killing of individual persons is forbidden. Some versions of the Bible must have put the sentence "You shall not murder" to say that since the law is Jewish, the law cannot include killing of animals and killing in war. It can only mean "you shall not kill individual human beings". This is true to the Jews.

However, we can still discuss that writers of the sixth law either be aware of or unaware of the Jewish situation stated above. It is known to us that different writers of the Bible often contradicted to each other on same topics. For example, there is contradiction between eating of meat and not eating of meat, and between clean and unclean animals. While some verses in Genesis 1 and Acts 10 seemed to claim that all kinds of animals are eatable, a passage in Leviticus 11 states that there are unclean animals too. While these passages allowed eating of meat of some kinds or of all kinds animals, Daniel 1, Isaiah 11, Romans 8:19ff seemed to say that meat eating should be avoided by more spiritual people, as a way of emphasizing salvation of the whole creation. By knowing such possible contradictions in the Bible, there is possibility to doubt the view that writer of the sixth law in the ten commandments fully remember the Jewish view of killing in war.

Our discussion shows us that according to the first view the law forbids all kinds of killings, such as killing of animals, killing in war, and killing of individuals. The second version means that what is forbidden is only killing of individual human beings apart from killing in war.

Whatever the case is, we are very sure that they are human made laws which may or may not resemble or be equivalent to unseen law of God. While the second version is more like the law of Israel, the first version appears to resemble the law of God more. This means that all the following kinds of killing, such as killing of individual human beings, killing of animals, insects, etc., and killing of enemies in war, are against the will of God. These two passages from the Pentateuch are few examples which have negative attitude to killing of one or of all kinds.

11

Negative Attitude to War/Killing in the Historical Books

Only few passages may suffice to discuss negative attitude to war or killing in the historical books.

11.1. God Rejected David's Plan to Build the Temple Because he shed too much Blood in Battles. *(I Chronicles 22:6-8).*

According to the writer (a writer) of I Chronicles,[9] David asked his son Solomon to build a house for the Lord, God of Israel. According to David or the writer, David was not allowed to build a house for the Lord, because although he had the mind to build a house for the Lord, the Lord could not allow him to do so as he shed too much blood and have made great wars.[10] It may be true to say that it was David's own guilt feeling, that he felt guilty for waging war too much. An ancient king of India called Ashoka the Great, once regretted, before he died, that he was greatly touched by the number of enemies he had killed, that he promised not to fight war again. King David too must have the same kind of regret that he fought so much war and thus shed so much blood. David must have the feeling that the Lord was not pleased with him for shedding so much blood. He must have made his feeling as if stated by the Lord, so that people may regard it as God's own saying.

Whatever it may be, it shows reader of the Bible that killing in war too is a crime, and as such a great sin. Since David was a good king, as much as king Ashoka was, he must be able to have this self condemnation of himself in killing so many people.

11.2. Prophet Micaiah Declared that God Would not Fight for Israel

According to the writer (or a writer) of I Kings,[11] while four hundred prophets, summoned by kings Ahab and Jehoshaphat, promised them that God would be with them if they would fight with the Syrians to regain Ramoth-gil-e-ad, another prophet called Micaiah declared that God would never fight with them in war with the Syrians.

A brief note on this incident need be discussed for our purpose. As was requested by king Jehoshaphat of Judah, King Ahab of Israel gathered four hundred prophets and asked them to consult God whether he would go to Ramoth-gil-e-ad to fight for the people of Israel against Ramoth-gilead. The prophets answered positively. They asked him to go to war with these people, for the Lord would deliver the city into the hands of the Kings. According to these prophets, the Lord would go with Israelites/ Jews in their war against that city.

However, there was another prophet whose name was called Micaiah. Probably he alone was true prophet at that time. According to Ahab, king of Israel, this prophet, Micaiah never prophesied any good thing for him (Ahab). He hated the prophet for this reason. It means that Micaiah never told him that God would go with him in war against other nations. Ahab often wanted to hear from Micaiah that God wanted to go with him (Ahab) in his war with other nations. Micaiah used to say the opposite. So, Ahab hated him for this. Since Jehoshaphat urged Ahab to ask Micaiah again whether God would allow him to fight with Syrians or not. As Ahab did so, Micaiah told him that he saw all Israel scattered on the mountain, as sheep that have no shepherd. He also said that the Lord told him that these have no master. Let each return to his house in peace. Micaiah was struck on the cheek by Zedekiah, the son of Chenaanah for saying the truth. Zedekiah questioned the way Micaiah received the words of the Lord. After king Ahab ordered his men to imprison Micaiah until he would return in peace, Micaiah still say that if Ahab and his men return in peace, it must be a proof that Micaiah never receive the words of the Lord. King Ahab died in that battle. According to the writer, prophet Micaiah was true prophet who did not hide the truth and did not pretend to support the king, but faced every confrontation.

According to our finding in this passage, the four hundred prophets gathered by Ahab (probably false prophets) promised Ahab that God permitted him (Ahab) to fight with the Syrians. However, Micaiah, (probably the one true prophet at that time), told Ahab the truth, that God would not go with him in his battle with Syrians for possession of the city of Ramonth Gilead. According to the passage, Micaiah'a prediction became true, while the prediction of the four hundred prophets was not true.

The passage should be understood in one of the following ways (a) According to Israelites' understanding of God's attitude to war, Micaiah's prophecy was situational. It is meant for that particular battle only. This means that God did not support the Israelites in their fight against other nations, particularly on this occasion only. At other times he used to support Israelites in their fight against other nations. (b) According to second view, it was only false prophets who used to say that God serves some time as captain of the army, or warrior, or often fight for Israelites. True Prophets never pretended to say in front of kings, that God used to go with Israelites in their battle with other nations.

(c) True prophets too so often claim that God used to support Israelites in their battle with other nations. This is not because whatever they say is true. But because they too used to have weaknesses. They often claim that God would support Israelites in their war with other nations, sometimes to please kings and people. They often do so also because they were not beyond the people. They used to have knowledge about this as much as the Israelites did. They too often made mistakes in claiming that God used to support the Israelites in war. It used to be only human views, that God involves himself in war between Israelites and other nations. God's purpose of choosing his people is to change the world by doing the best to all. It is the opposite of God's will to fight enemies all the times.

Endnotes

9. I Chronicles 22:6-8.
10. I Chronicles 22:8.
11. I Kings 22:1 28.

12

Negative Attitude to War/Killing in the Book of Proverbs

Out of the Poetical and Wisdom books, some verses in the book of the Proverbs are chosen to discuss something against war and killing.

12.1. Do not Rejoice when Your Enemy Falls (Prov. 24:17-18)

This sentence carries a note of recognition of the presence of the enemies. However, it goes much beyond the Israelite's view of war and defeat in wars. Although, it is not a direct statement of not to fight wars/battles, it is a note of an advanced life in which there would be no more war. This advice is an advice to mature Israelites not to be rejoiced even when enemy falls. Those who believed in war and those who love to wage war used to be happy when enemies fall. Those who feel sad when enemies fall must be the people who love enemies. So, the advice not to be rejoiced "when enemy falls" is a way of life beyond war and violence. The following sentences may be compared to each other in order to find out the standard of the advice.

1. Kill all the enemies
2. Be happy when the enemy falls.
3. Do not rejoice when your enemy falls
4. Love your enemies.

5. Give food to your hungry enemy and water to your thirsty enemy

These five lines may be taken as five laws for this chapter. The first law

"Kill all your enemies" is a way of life of the Israelites in ancient Israel.

Israelites have no love at all for enemies, nor do they have any mercy for them. So, the law here, "Kill all the enemies" is the standard of life for these war loving people.

The second law, "be happy when the enemy falls" above, does not go beyond the first law. It is the nature of war above, Do not rejoice when your enemy falls is the standard of life of a much more advanced people. It is a step or move away from standard of life of war loving people like the Israelites. It is a way to come out of war loving situations. It is a means to come out of evil societies which love war with enemies. Therefore let it be taken as an advice to come out of a low standard of life under war, violence or killings. It is a means to come out of low standard of living. The fifth law above "Give food to your hungry enemy" (which will be dealt below), is a fitting standard of life of those who already came out of war loving society. Such a standard of life will slowly extinguish the fire of enmity between nations. It is a practical application of the advice "to love one's enemy".

The second phrase in the same verse[12] "and do not let your heart be glad when he (your enemy) stumbles" does not go beyond the first phrase, "Do not rejoice when your enemy falls".

12.2. If Your Enemy is Hungry give him Bread to Eat (Prov. 25:21-22)

To give bread to one's hungry enemy is impossible for those who strongly feel the presence of enemies. There must be possible fear of death too. To do so, one may be afraid that the enemy would take a chance to attack or harm us. During communal clashes in our area, there was fear of enemies. In such a situation, who would dare to give food to hungry enemies? So, in such a situation the advice seems to be an impossible one.

However, it is possible to think that this advice is not only to avoid war or enmity, but even to eliminate enmities, violence, war etc. It is not impossible to give food to the hungry enemy and water to the thirsty enemy. It is not possible for those who hate enemies. It is impossible for those who cannot forgive mistakes or harms done to us by enemies. It is impossible to give food and water to one's hungry and thirsty enemies for those who have no love.

So, to love the enemy is one key to give food and water to one's hungry and thirsty enemy. Without love one cannot forgive one's enemy. The purpose of giving food to the hungry and water to the thirsty enemy is to be seen from the sentence "For so you will heap burning coals on his head, and the Lord will reward you."[13] This sentence can be taken to mean that by giving food to the hungry enemy and water to the thirsty enemy, there will be change of life in the life of the enemy. This unexpected goodness will cause shame in the feeling of the enemy and have change of life in him/her. This extraordinary goodness to one's enemy would become instrumental to change the lives of the enemies. It is a wonderful means to change the world.

If this be the will of God, God must have hated war and killing, and violence of any kind. The God who wills this extraordinary goodness would never allow hatred, violence, communal clashes, war between nations. It must not be God who allows war between nations. It must be writers of the Bible or the people of the time who claimed that God often participated in Israelites' wars against nations. God who is extraordinarily good to human beings cannot allow war/killings between nations. The wise man whose view is in this particular proverb must be chosen by God than earlier Israelites who never fully know the will of God. The will of God is to choose his people to change the world by doing good to all. It is human view only to say that God used to fight with other nations through the Israelites.

12.3. The Murderer is Digging his/her Own Grave Before he/she Dies

This sentence shows strong apposition to murder, i.e. killing of individuals. It is also a warning not to kill. It also seemed to have the law, "A tooth for a tooth and an eye for an eye", in its background. The sentence appears more irony than the sixth commandment, "You shall not murder".

The proverb seems to imply that the murderer will die soon, depending on the law of retaliation with limitation, "tooth for a tooth and an eye for an eye". In the world of lawlessness too murderers cannot survive so long. War lovers will die of war, killers will be killed by others. Even Jesus said," He who use sword will die of sword. He/she must die sooner or later. An Israelite may or may not take stoning a man/woman to death for adultery or other sins as murder. While a Jew/Israelite allows stoning a man/woman to death for his/her sin, murder is forbidden. For God, both of them may be similarly sinful.

Passages chosen from the book of Proverbs may be summarized as follow. Murder is sin. Murderers must be aware that they must die early. So, any one should avoid murder. We must even try not to have enemy. A man/woman may unwillingly have enemy. In such a situation too, a man/woman of God should not rejoice when one's enemy falls. One should rather feed one's hungry and thirsty enemy. So, that he may change his/her life as a part of changing the world. Because the purpose of our calling is to change the world by doing the best to one's enemies. Those who plan to destroy enemies do not know God.

Endnotes

12. Proverbs 24:17.
13. Proverbs 25:22.

13

Negative Attitude to War/Killing in the Prophetic Books

Among the books of the prophets some passages from the Book of Isaiah and the Book of Jonah may be chosen to show that war used to be a way of dealing with other nations according to the understanding of Israelites, but not according to the will of the Lord.

13.1. Isaiah's Vision of Life in the Future Messianic Age

According to prophet Isaiah,[14] the earth will be full of knowledge of God as much as water fills the Oceans, when the Messiah, who is described as a shoot from the stump of Jesse, comes. At that time the Messiah will rule with righteousness. Under his rule all fierce animals will no more harm meek animals. All must become friends because of the new knowledge of God through the Messiah. The characteristic of the arrival of the Messiah must be peaceful-co-existence of all living beings, including trees. Peaceful co-existence of all living beings is the will of God to be practiced by God's creatures. Since peaceful co-existence is the goal of perfection, and since it is the will of God, the opposite of this, i.e., violence, killing and war cannot and would never be encouraged by God. It might be the claim of false teachings in the Old Testament that God encouraged war between nations.

13.2. Isaiah's Idea of the Suffering Servant

Prophet Isaiah speaks of the Messiah as the suffering Servant.[15] He is despised and rejected by men. He has born our griefs and carried our sorrows. This suffering of the suffering servant is not a pretension, nor is it a dramatic event. It is possible because he did not resist evil for evil, he used non-violence, he was meek. It is caused both by the wickedness of the people and by the non-resistance of the servant. Isaiah did not state this simply to keep the record of it. He must have stated it to be an example of life for God's people. And as such, all people of God are supposed to be willing to suffer in the name of the Lord for others. If at all it be an example for the pattern of life for the people of God, then there must be no place for war and violence in the lives of God's people.

Christians are supposed to live like him, by being non-resistant. This should not be an alternative way of life. Rather it should be the only way of life of the true people of God. This shows us the fact that violence and war could be present in the lives of wicked nations only. There can be no place for violence and war in the lives of the disciples of the Suffering Servant. What is more powerful than non-resistance is humility, meekness, and willingness to suffer.

13.3. Jonah's Mission to Nineveh

The book of Jonah tells us that Jonah was sent to the city of Nineveh, a gentile city, to preach the good tidings. Due to his Jewish mindedness against gentiles, he was very selfish to go to Nineveh to spread the good news. The writer wanted to say that God continue to call him and sent him to Nineveh, to preach the good tidings. He was protected in the belly of the big fish. After he came out of the belly of the big fish, he agreed with the proposal and he went to Nineveh. As he preached the good tidings, the whole city began to repent of their sins.

The writer wanted to show us that God loves Gentiles as much as he loves Jews. He loves all human beings at the same level. Therefore, it is wrong to say that God used to fight for Israel in their wars against other nations. God is not the God of one nation. He is the God of all nations. So, he cannot be convinced to fight for one nation against other nations. God is not a partial God nor was he a selfish God. He loves and cares for all. He cannot be happy when nations fight each other.

Our study of the books of the prophets shows us the fact that there is no place for war in the life of the people of God. Christians who are supposed to have peaceful co-existence with each other and peaceful co-existence with all animals have no place for violence, killing or war in their lives. God is God of justice and he has nothing to do with national and international differences. War has no place in his agenda.

Passages chosen from the prophetic books show us the fact that the will of God is not only to preach the good news to the gentile nations, but even to animals and other creatures and have unbroken peace with them. To have such a perfect peace with the whole creation is not to create or invent a new thing on earth. Rather it is a restoration of the original state of life in the whole universe, and as a restoration of God's good creation.

Permission for war in the Old Testament was based on some wrong views on God in relation to Gentiles. First of all it was based on misunderstanding of God's election of Israel. God might not choose Israel as a nation. He could have chosen Abraham, Joseph, Moses Joshua, Samuel, David, Solomon, etc. However, he might not have especially chosen Israel. Even if he has chosen Israel separately, he must have chosen them to be light to the world, Salt of the earth, but not be bitterness in the world. So, the second basis for Israelites' wrong understanding of God's relation to them is their misunderstanding of their mission to the world. Believers are chosen to spread the good news to the world. The Book of Jonah correctly shows us the fact that while God loves gentiles too as much as he loves the Israelites, Israelites forgot this attitude of God and hated gentiles. So, they wrongly fought war with other nations and wrongly thought that even God fought war for them, with them or at least allow them to fight gentile nations. Thus, they so often told lie that God used to go with them in war against other nations.

Endnotes

14. Isaiah 11:1 – 9.

15. Isaiah 53:1 - 12.

14

Negative Attitude to War/Killing in the Teachings of Jesus

As Christians we believed that Jesus Christ is the self-revelation of God. According to this we can know God through Jesus Christ. It also means that if we can know the life, works, teachings and mind of Jesus, we can know God somehow. This is true in Paul's Theology. For Paul Jesus Christ is the image of the invisible God![16] Jesus said, "He who has seen me has seen the Father.[17] From these two verses we are able to say that by knowing Jesus more closely, we can know God better. Accordingly we can have a study of the will of God about war and peace, through the life, works and teachings of Jesus. By choosing some important teachings, life and works of Jesus, we may have a study of the Will of God regarding War and Killing.

14.1. The Law of Non-Resistance

Against the Law of limited retaliation in the Old Testament[18] "a tooth for a tooth and an eye for an eye", Jesus put a new law of non-resistance, "Do not resist an evil doer."[19] In the Old Testament there was permission for limited retaliation, "to take revenge for as much as one receives". Literally it means that if a man broke a tooth of another man, this other man would be allowed to break a tooth of the man who broke his tooth, but no more. If a father hurt the eye of a young man, that young man has the right to hurt the eye of that father. More than this, suppose there is no law to avoid retaliation, and that everyone would be allowed to take as much revenge as possible. Under such freedom of retaliation, it could be possible in some countries to kill each other and finish each other. So, even permission to have limited retaliation is no more appreciable.

The words of Jesus are even more than not to take revenge. The idea of non-resistance of evil is more than just to avoid retaliation". "Not to resist evil," may even connote in it the idea of allowing oneself to be persecuted or beaten. Earliest Christians could bear persecutions in the name of Christ. Jesus also added, (Rather), "If someone strikes (slaps) your right cheek, turn to him your left (check) too."[20] If someone persecutes Christians, they are supposed to allow or give room to the persecutors to persecute them even more, instead of resisting. The following two versions of the sentence too need to be compared:

Do not resist evil doer.
Do not resist evil.

The first translation appears to be a commentary. However, what we are to resist here is not the evil doer, but the evil itself. There cannot be an evil without the doer. However, it is good to note that what Christians are not to resist is not the evil itself, but the evil doer.

The disciples of Jesus are supposed to allow themselves to be persecuted. In such a situation there is no room for war and killing in the lives of the people of God. If Christians are supposed to be like this, it is not wrong to say that Christians should not participate in wars and killings .War cannot be a part of Christians' life. (Mathew 5:39)

14.2. Do Not be Angry without a Cause (Matt. 5:22)

Some of the sayings of Jesus appeared to be much away from the Jewish laws quoted by him. While the law of non-resistance is much away from the Jewish law "a tooth for a tooth and an eye for an eye", the advice "not to be angry "is too much steps away from the Jewish law "you shall not murder", For a man/woman whose nature is still un-regenerated, there is possibility to kill someone who is believed to be an enemy to someone. In other words, if there be a possible cause, an unregenerated man/woman has a tendency to kill someone. For Jesus, anger is a possible spark of murder. Where there is no anger, there cannot be murder or killing in war. Since Jesus knew all these, he talked of avoiding the spark of murder, i.e., anger. Therefore the best way not to murder is to totally avoid anger; in order for a man/woman to be totally free from anger it is necessary to have a regenerated life. For Paul" to be in Christ" is a means to avoid anger. It is not enough to avoid anger. It is necessary to be free from anger. Many people still feel happy if someone whom they hated is being killed by someone else. Jesus wanted all human beings to be free from this wish for the death of one's hated ones. If a man/woman knows no anger, or cannot be angry to cause evil, he/she cannot think of killing someone. If a nation has no anger against other nations, there cannot be war. So, to Jesus, the spark or cause of murder and killing in war is anger. Therefore, for Jesus the law "not to murder" is not enough, because just to abstain from murder implies that anger is still in the mind. In the Jewish context, laws are made against existing sins. As much as the law "Do not steal" is necessary law for thieves, the law "Do not murder" is necessary law among killers or murderers. But if these murderers are given this law "you shall not murder," they need to put their anger under a cover in their minds/hearts. However, among those who know no anger the law "not to murder" is not a necessary law. As much as fire cannot be started without a spark, there cannot be murder and killing in war without anger in any one. So, a new advice of Jesus "Do not be angry" is a means to avoid all kinds of violence, communal clashes, murder, war, etc.

Jesus was very careful enough to add "a cause" in his new advice. So, his advice becomes "Do not be angry without a cause". This, however, permitted anger in some other situations. A man/woman is allowed to be angry against all evils in the world, but not against any human being.

14.3. Forgive One Another

In a society where there is no untoward attitude to each other, there is nothing to forgive each other. However, in a society where there are so much wrong relationships either between individuals or between groups, one key to reduce or remove fightings, clashes, killings, war, etc is to forgive each other. Without forgiveness some social ills cannot be healed. Forgiveness is the key to open the door to good relationships. It is a medicine to heal some social illnesses. Forgiveness is the key to keep peace in the world too. If countries have the necessary quality to forgive each other, there cannot be any war between each other. So, forgiveness is a key to peace in the world too.

If a country is good enough to forgive another country's mistake, there would be peace between the two countries. So, if all countries are good enough to forgive the possible mistakes of other countries, there will be real peace in the world. Thus, forgiveness is a good key to international peace. There cannot be any war between countries who have this good quality to forgive each other.

For Jesus, Christian forgiveness should be limitless. Jesus says that one should forgive others 7 times 70 (7 x 70 = 490). Everyone knows the fact that no one can have this much mistakes. Even if we take all the mistakes of neighbours against one neighbour together, the total cannot even reach single 70. Therefore, to forgive 7 times 70 or 490 times means to forgive others without any limit. It is to forgive others without remembering earlier mistakes.

It is to forgive others without counting the number of mistakes of one person against him/her. It also means that if a person commits a fourth mistake against you, you should forgive him as if it is the first sin, by not counting earlier three mistakes. If this kind of forgiveness is in every one in the world, wars and killings, violence, etc will have no place in the world.

It is, then, understandable to all that the God who always have good–will for the world, must never fight war for Israel against other nations. Although, God may have some changes in other areas, he never changes in principle. God always wants his people to forgive each other. He never encourages any nation to fight with other nations. It is based on **LIE** to say that God used to fight wars for Israel against other nations.

14.4. Love Your Neighbour as you Love Yourself

There may be two different ways of understanding neighbours. One is Jesus' view of neighbour. We may want to give more meaning to the idea of neighbour than it was in the mind of Jesus. It does not mean that ours is right and that of Jesus is wrong. It only means that due to change of situations, our view of "neighbour" may have more meanings. (a) In a narrow sense people living around our homes (b) If the good Samaritan in a parable of Jesus would be the neighbour of the wounded man, then neighbour would mean those who are good to us, those who could help us, those who could meet our needs, etc.

(c) In a wider sense any human being could be our neighbour. All human beings may possibly be our neighbour today. (d) In the world of ecological crisis today everything around us may be our neighbours. For example, the air we breathe, the atmosphere around us, the forest around us, animals, the waters we used to drink, the soil in which we used to grow our food producing plants, etc. While human beings are our wicked neigbours these neighbours are our good neighbours.

It is too narrow to talk of "our neighbours" as people living around our homes. Jesus was believed to refer to anyone who do good to others, as our neighbours. All those who believed God too may be our neighbours in a sense. It is not so easy to do good to others. If we take "neighbours" in this sense, some people who live very close to our homes may not be our neighbours.

Today our neighbours could include all human beings. Jesus may not object to the idea that neighbours include all human beings. If all human beings are our neighbours, they are so much. Can we really love all human beings as our neighbours? The answer is, if we have love, we can love all human beings in one sense. But if we do not have love, we cannot love even one man/woman. So, the answer depends on whether we have love or not. If we have the love called **agape** we must be able to love all human beings. If we are able to love all we have no place for enmity and war between us. Since to love all human beings is the will of God, there can be no place for killings, war, clashes, in the mind of God. God can never allow violence, war and killing of any kind in the world.

If Jesus happened to discuss this question with us, he may not reject the view that "Our neighbour "today includes the whole creation. If I think for Jesus, there is nothing for him to disagree with the view that our neighbours refers to all human beings and the whole creation. It is God's will for Christians to love all human beings and the whole creation as well. The purpose is to bring back peace and harmony in the world at large in the whole universe. Within such a purpose there cannot be room for violence, killing or wars, which are results of human sinfulness. They should not be taken to be used by or allowed by God. Everyone should now agree to say that Israelites wrongly believed in God's involvement in war and God's support of Israelites in their fighting against enemies. War is not the norm of life of Christians. But love could be the norm of life of Christians. Where there is love there cannot be hatred, violence, retaliation, war and killing of any kind. War cannot be allowed among those who have love as the norm of life.

But the problem is the possibility of loving others as much as we love ourselves. All human beings would say that no one can love others, as much as he/she loves himself/herself. The possibility may be there only when everyone realize the fact that all human beings are brothers and sisters. At such a time there cannot be any untoward attitude to each other and thus war and violence cannot have any room among brothers and sisters.

14.5. Do to Others What You Wish them Done to You

The golden rule "Do to others what you wish them done to you" is a standard of life in the kingdom of God. It is in opposition to negative laws. Negative laws are meant to restrain wicked people. On the other hand the golden rule is a pattern of life to be followed by good and obedient people who would be willing to follow any good advice.

If and since the golden rule is the pattern of life for the people of God, war, killing, violence, etc can never be adviced or accepted by God for his people. The God who accepted the golden rule to be a way of life of his people, cannot allow, communal clashes, violence, murder, war, etc. among his people.

If and since the golden rule is the pattern of life for the people of God, war, killing, violence, etc can never be advised or accepted by God for his people. The God who accepted the golden rule to be a way of life of his people, cannot allow, communal clashes, violence, murder, war, etc. among his people. Therefore, if Israelites would be the people of God, the one who encouraged them to go to war against other nations cannot be this God. It must have been the view of Israelites themselves.

14.6. He/She Who Wish to be the Greatest Must be Servant of All

Nobody seems to dislike to be in the highest position in the society or in the state or in the world. Everyone likes to be the greatest. Alexander the Great, Hitler, Nepoleon, all wanted to be the greatest in the world. Each of them tried to become the greatest by suppressing or subdueing others. Everyone tries to be the greatest in the world. James and John too tried to become the greatest in the kingdom of God by asking the positions from Jesus. However, Jesus told them to first become servant of all. This is the right way or means to become the greatest.

War too seems to be the way or means to become greater than others by suppressing others. But war is an evil and wrong means to become the greatest. It is not the Christian way in the world of human beings. Any Christian too can become the greatest in the world if one follows the right means or ways. Jesus asked his disciples to be servant of all so that they may become the greatest. The way "servant of all" is the way or means to become the greatest not only in the world of religions, but also in the secular world. Those who follow this way do not need to follow the way of war and killing. Christians who follow this way may hate to follow the way of war and killing. Christians who follow the way of war may not be followers of Jesus. The way of war may be a weak means to humiliate others. The way of "Servant of all' may be the stronger or even the strongest weapon to humiliate others and even to win all for Christ. For those who love the way laid down by Jesus, war may appear to be an evil way.

14.7. Love Your Enemies

Jesus asked his disciples to love their enemies. If Christians are right in claiming that Jesus is the revelation of God or that God revealed himself through Jesus Christ, he must be the revealer of the will of God too. If so, his advice to love the enemies must be the will also of God. If this be true, it could not be God who advised Israelites to wage war against other nations. It is now certain that it was the Israelites who themselves claimed that God fought for Israel, God fought other nations through war.

To love one's enemy seems to be an impossible advice. However, the problem is not the possibility or impossibility to love enemies. Rather, it is the question whether we have this love or not. If we have this love, we must love. Since it is Jesus' advice to love the enemies, God must have wished to tell the same advice to ancient Israelites. The problem must be the greater gap between God and ancient Israelites. If God would wish to give the same advice to the ancient Israelites, he must have never told them to wage war against enemies. It is even funny to read a verse or to mention that God asked Israelites to wage war against other nations.

14.8. Jesus Attitude to Peter's Use of Sword

At the place of the arrest of Jesus Peter tried to defend his Lord with his sword. He drew out his sword and cut the ear of one of those who came to arrest him at the garden of Gethsemane. The man he cut at the ear was a servant of the high Priest called Malcus. However, Jesus did not support his defender and rather said, "Put your sword into the sheath"[21]..."for all who take the sword will perish by the sword."[22] It is true to say that no human being would be able to say to his defender what Jesus said to Peter here. Even in front of death Jesus was able to follow the will of God.

Jesus did not only live his own life. He lives the life according to the will of God. No fear of death diverted his course of life nor did it win Jesus to choose something against God's will. Since, Jesus was a non-violent being, he could not live the way of violence. To live a violent life may meant to live against the will of God. So, we can say that non-violence is a permanent principle of God, and so Jesus could not choose another way. If so, (a) it must be wrong to claim that God used to initiate Israelites' war with other nations. (b) It is also wrong to say that God is captain of the army of Israel, or warrior. (c) It is also wrong to claim that God used to fight war for Israel against other nations. It is funny human imagination that God allowed Israelites to fight war with other nations. It is wrong to say that a non-violent God used violence in the time of the Old Testament.

14.9. The Silence of Jesus in Front of the High Priest and Pilate

Christians claimed that God is most powerful; he can do everything which are allowed within his own self limitation. So, if violence is the way of God, he would have protected Jesus in front of the High Priest and Pilate, by using any possible means. If ancient Israelites were right in claiming that God is a violent God, involving himself in Israelites' war against other nations, he must have protected Jesus in front of those who arrested him, and in front of the High Priests and Pilate. However, Jesus' use of non-violence/non-resistance in front of these people, shows that God must not be involved himself in wars between Israelites and their enemies. It is wrong to say that God is black in the Old Testament but white in the New Testament. We can infer that as much as Jesus did not use violence anywhere at difficult situations, God must be a non-violent God, and thus it is pure lie to claim that he involved himself in wars, in the Old Testament times.

14.10. The Death of Jesus on the Cross

The death of Jesus could be the apex of his non-violence. Why did Jesus die on the cross? This question can be answered in some different ways.

(a) Because it was apart of the salvafic work of God. (b) because the Jewish fundamentalist wanted him death as a result of their hatred against him. (c) Because it was a Roman way of torturing criminals. Because, he was condemned as a criminal. (d) Because Jesus is the suffering servant. He suffered like a meek man/woman in the midst of wicked people. (e) Jesus suffered on the cross because of his non-vilent/non-resistant way of living. So, the cross is the zenith of the violent/nonresistant means of Jesus. Since Jesus is the self-revelation of God, the non-violent/non-resistant way of life of Jesus shows the fact that God is a non-violent/non-resistant God, since the beginning of time. He is a non-violent God from the very beginning. Jesus reveals this fact. He cannot be a violent God once, in the Old Testament time, and became a non-violent God in the New Testament time.

No. It is wrong to say like this. What is wrong is that people in the Old Testament time did not know him as he is. They wrongly knew him. They wrongly understood him to be a violent God, a war loving God, a God who retaliates. Jesus really revealed it to us that God is a non-violent God, from the very beginning. It is wrong to claim that this non-violent God was violent in the time of the Old Testament, and was described as warrior, captain of the army, etc., in the Old Testament time. To say like this is to ignorantly tell lie.

14.11. Jesus Christ as Peace Maker

Christians partly accepted Jesus as peace Maker. As Christians we verbally or theoretically accepted the view that he is peace Maker, but not fully or practically. This means that, although we used to choose sermon topics like "Prince of Peace", Peace through Jesus Christ, "Shalom", etc., during Christmas seasons, and Good Friday seasons, our Christian lives do not show any such peace to the world. Christians waged wars, produced arms and ammunitions, weapons of mass destruction, war planes more than non-Christians. Christians participated in the arms race of all nations. This means that most Christians do not know who Jesus is. So, we need to tell Christians today again that Jesus is peace Maker.

In order to know Jesus Christ as Peace Maker, we must not only see the New Testament passages which may be used as such. Prophet Isaiah foretold the birth of a future king who would be called the Prince of Peace.[23] Christians believed that he must have been the Messiah. He must be the one from God whose reign would be filled with peace. He must show forth the true nature of God. Since he would be called prince of peace, one can rightly infer that God is the God of peace, but not the God of war and killing. Because – (a) he must reign as the representative of God. He must reign as God reigns. This is to prove that by Jesus and through his reign as prince of peace, God must have been king of peace, but not of war and conflict.

(b) Through the prince of peace we can know God as he really is. Since Israelites misunderstood the true nature of God, they talked of him as warrior; captain of the army, one who lead the army in their wars against other nations. The birth and work of the prince of peace would reveal that God is the God of peace. The prince of peace will unveil that Israelites misunderstood God and thus wrongly described him as warrior, initiator of war with enemies, captain of the army, etc. The birth of the prince of peace will become an opener, to open our eyes to see that God is not the God of war, rather he is the God of peace. Israelites blindly mislead the world to think that God is a fighting God, rather than a peaceful God. So, the birth of the Prince of peace must correct our understanding of God as God of war. Now, the birth of the Messiah will tell us the fact that God is the God of peace who never allow war between Israelites and other nations.

Jesus' work of peace is symbolically explained by the fact that the veil in the temple was torn into two,[24] as soon as Jesus died on the Cross. The veil in the temple was a partition between Jews and gentiles. So, the fact that the veil was torn into two symbolized the removal of the partition between the two groups. It symbolically showed the removal or destruction of all kinds of differences, sectarianism, caste and classes. It symbolized the work of Jesus as peace maker between nations, enemies, groups, individuals, etc. His death on the cross symbolized destruction of all forces of enmities, differences, groupism, sectarianism even to bring lasting peace in the world. In doing so, Jesus did not do anything against the Father He was only fulfilling eternal divine will on the cross. It thus served as a destruction and correction of the Jewish wrong understanding of God as warrior who fought for Israel against other nations, captain of the army who led people of Israel in war with other nations. The work of Jesus on the cross is a symbolical destruction of all kinds of enmity between nations and between human beings and God. The work of Jesus on the cross is a symbolical destruction not only of partition walls between nations, but even to destroy Jewish view of God hating other nations and thus involved himself in Israelites' war against other nations. The work of Jesus did not change God's attitude to other nations. Rather, it reveals Jewish wrong understanding of God as choosing Israelites to destroy others. This wrong view about God in the life of the Israelite/Jews may gradually be removed with better and better knowledge of the works and life of Jesus.

Our study of the life, teachings and works of Jesus shows us the fact that God must be a peace loving God, God of peace who hated war between nations, not only now, but from the very beginning. This is revealed by the life and works of Jesus. The death of Jesus on the cross especially revealed the non-resistant ways of God. It is not only the way of Jesus, but mainly the way of God. Therefore, we now realize that the ancient Israelites' view of God as warrior, or captain of the army of Israel was baseless. It was based on wrong concepts of Israel.

Endnotes

16. Colossians 1:15a.
17. John 14:9.
18. Exodus 21:24; Leviticus 24:20; Deut. 19:21.
19. Matthew 5:38.
20. Matthew 5:39.
21. John 18:10, 11.
22. Matthew 26:52.
23. Isaiah 9:6.
24. Luke 23:45.

15

Negative Attitude to War/Killing in other Books of the New Testament

One passage, probably quoted from an Old Testament passage, is chosen from Romans to emphasize the purpose of the Gospel as a work of peace, and not a work of waging war.

15.1. Giving the Need of the Enemy (Romans 12:20)

Paul must have quoted his idea of giving food to the hungry enemy and water to a thirsty enemy[25] from Proverbs.[26] This has already been described in section 12.2. The idea of giving bread (food) to the hungry enemy and water to the thirsty enemy sounds to be an advice to achieve an impossible task. However, the idea of giving food to the hungry enemy is one of the best works a Christian could achieve.

Giving food to the hungry enemy and giving water to the thirsty enemy may have similar difficulties and similar good results as well. They need not be discussed separately.

The status or standard of this advice may be measured by comparing the following terms:

(1) The law of retaliation
(2) The law of limited retaliation
(3) Non-violence
(4) Non-resistance
(5) Doing good to our neighbours
(6) Doing the best to enemies
(Give food to your hungry enemy).

According to the above table, the standard of non-violence (No (3) above) is higher than those of Nos 1 & 2 above. The law of non-résistance is much higher to that of the law of non-violence. Moreover, our present discussion on No (6). "Give food and water to the hungry and thirsty enemy" is much better than No (5), "doing good to our neighbours". Therefore, we can say that doing the best to one's enemy is one of the best works in Christian life. Doing well to one's relatives is far below "doing the best to one's enemies". It is one of the best ways for individuals to make peace with enemies. It is not only to make peace with enemies, but even to help one's enemy change his/'her life, or their lives.

The purpose of the advice to do good to one's enemy, is to be seen in the next line, "for in so doing you will heap burning coals on his head." It is believable that although it appears to be very difficult to do such good works to enemies, to be able to do such good works to enemies must do some thing to change his/her life. "Heap charcoals of fire" may mean to make him/her feel ashame and thus change his/her life." Extremely good works are supposed to win the hearts of many, even of enemies, and thus convert them in one way or the other.

The God who advises his people to love enemies and to fulfill this love by means of good work wishes good-will to all human beings. This advice to do good to enemies is fitting to be the will of God who loves all people of all nations. Therefore, the view that "God wished Israelites to destroy the enemies" cannot be fitted to the will of God. God is not: the God of war, "nor is he the "warrior", nor the "Captain of the army." Rather he loves both Israelites and Gentiles at the same time. God always loves enemies of Israelites, but does not hate the Israelites. He loves both at equal level.

15.2. The Message of Peace

Peace is a part of the Gospel message, because God is God of peace. The Gospel is the gospel of peace and not of war. This gospel belongs to God. Therefore, God could never be a warrior, nor captain of the army of Israel, who took initiative of wars. As much as Jesus is the Prince of peace, God must be the God of peace. He can never be God of war, nor God of violence. Paul's idea of reconciliation does not only refer to human beings' reconciliation to God, but also reconciliation and peace between individual human beings, peace between nations, peace between groups or organizations, etc. Since God is the God of peace, he did not wait forever for human beings to reconcile to him. He took the initiative to bridge peace between him and human beings, and between human beings and human beings.

Although, there is no direct and systematic debate against Old Testament view of God waging physical war for Israel against other nations, no New Testament writer is believe to support the view that God is the God of war, captain of the army, warrior, one who took initiative in Israelites' war against other nations. This shows that there is the realization that God is God of peace and not of war. The gospel is the gospel of peace and the owner is the God of peace, who must never allow and appreciate war between nations.

Endnotes

25. Romans 12:20.
26. Proverbs 25:21,22.

16

Bad Effects of War/Killing

War used to have so many bad effects. It may be death, physical damage, psychological, mental spiritual, effects. These effects need be discussed briefly.

16.1. Physical Effects

Every historical war has physical effects. Thousands and millions of people died in world wars and other major wars. Costs of buildings destroyed, costs of weapons damaged, and ammunitions used cannot be counted. Damages made by atom bombs used in Japan during the World War II could not be counted. Costs of food supplies during the wars cannot be counted.

16.2. Untold Miseries

Major wars used to leave untold miseries due to properties damaged, lives lost, many left mained, many left in poverty, many left with fear psychosis. People killed in wars cannot be selective. Half of members of a family may sometimes die in some wars. In other wars whole families could die too. Such cases used to cause untold sorrows and miseries in the families. Some may loss costly and big buildings which the family may not be able to regain within many years.

16.3. Broken Relationships

War used to destroy national or international relationships. A mere enmity between two nations used to become much widened as a result of war between them. War used to leave nations' relationships broken for decades and even centuries. In such situations, each nation used to watch each other's movements and actions with suspicious eyes. Forgiveness used to be a forgotten quality.

16.4. War Retards Expansion of Christianity

Jesus knew that non-résistance is a means to spread the good news. The Good News too could be spread by means of doing good works to enemies. War is the opposite of these means of spreading the good news. Therefore, war not only weaken the spread of the gospel, but also retarded its spread.

A Christian is supposed to use non-resistance (which seems to be much stronger than non-violence), and doing good to one's enemy, as means to extend Christianity. So, war and violence are enemies of the gospel. Any disciple of Jesus should think that those who use violence and war are enemies of the Gospel.

However, if a Christian country used to wage war against people of other religions, that country prevented or retarded the growth of Christianity. In the Old Testament there is a claim that due to the sinfulness and wickedness of Israelites, people of other faiths used to condemn or reject the God of Israel. But, when they perform extraordinarily good works, many would begin to accept the God of Israel. Christians are supposed to shine in the world as light of the world. However, if they use war as a means to win other nations they are driving them away from Christianity. Instead of using the laws of non-resistance (as fought by Jesus) and the principle of feeding hungry enemies, Christian countries use war as a means to win others. Winning others by means of non-resistance and by means of feeding hungry enemies, Christians would become light in the darkness or it would serve as a means of removing darkness. But use of war and military power to win other nations must be likened to darkness overshadowing or driving away light.

16.5. To use War is to Conform to the World

Paul urges Christians not to be conformed to the ways of this world. In order to be transformed from the ways of the world, they need to be transformed from their inner beings.[27] This transformation must be a means not to conform to these ways of the world.

War is not a Christian way. It is a way of non Christians. If Christians use wars and killings they are conforming themselves to the ways of the world. Christians totally conformed themselves to the ways of the world mainly because they follow the wrong ways of the Israelites. Today it is next to impossibility to call out Christians from following this ways of the world. How can a man from a third world country convince a first world country to come out of the world's way of using weapons, violence or war? It cannot easily be possible.

War has many bad effects. One of the worst effects is to be finally conformed to the world's way of war to the extent that they are no more different from a polar bear in the midst of ice bergs or ice boulders. This means that Christians who choose the way of war become like the worldly people as a result of which they are no more different from them. War is a way of life of worldly people. Since Christians too follow this broad way, they are no more different from the worldly people. Paul may refer to our world today as "The lost world."

Endnotes

27. Romans 12 :2.

PART-3

A THEOLOGICAL REFLECTION ON WAR AND PEACE

It is very vital for us to produce a systematized or new theology on war and peace which may be convincing, understandable and acceptable to lay Christians, military personnel, government officers, philosophers, scientists, non-Christians etc. It should not only be a talk on the topics of peace and war. Theology of peace must be based on the nature of God and the true relationships of human beings. Some important bases for peace are chosen on the nature of God and human relationships.

17

The Love and Care of the Creator and Saviour of the World

Someone may surprise us to choose this designations of God in talking about war and peace.

However, these two designations are chosen because I believed that Christians' involvement in war or gun culture is traditionally inherited from Israelites' wrong belief in war as initiated and use by God. And Israelites' claim for God's participation in war is a wrong view of God, and their wrong view of God's election. So, we need to have a theology of peace based on God as Creator and Saviour of the world.

It is inferable to all the right thinking people that Creator of everything cannot be a war loving God. He must be a peace loving God. He must not only wish to keep peace in his created world, but even work for the restoration of peace in the caostic world.

We suppose that the claim of a writer of Genesis for God making human beings in his own images is true. We also agree that this image of God in human beings is not totally destroyed as a result of sin. This means that sin does not totally destroy image of God in each man/woman as a result of his/her sin or sins. Sin only disfigured or partly distorted this image of God in man/woman. Therefore, every human being has either partial (or full) image of God in him/her. As much as a writer loves the book he has written and he is much more related to the book than anyone else, God, as Creator of everything must love everything he has created, and is much related to everyone. A book reflects or shows forth the mind and understanding of the writer. Even if someone argues the points he/she has put forth in the book, he/she used to defend them. In the same way God as the Creator of everything is the author of human beings. He put his image in every man/woman. Therefore, it is true to say that God loves every one he has created, even after they might have committed sin. Since everyone continues to be made in his own image, he continues to be their Creator, and thus cannot break his relationship with human beings. God's image is always reflected in human beings, and they never ceased to be images of God. Therefore, it is wrong to think of God hating some one, i.e., gentiles, while he loves Israelites. It is totally wrong to think of God fighting war for Israel against gentile nations. God is Creator both of Jews and Gentiles. He cannot love one alone but hate the other. He cannot hate gentiles while loving Jews.

It is sometimes true to say that some parents used to love one or two particular child/children but hated some of their children. However, God should not be taken as a wicked father or mother like them. God has no partiality. He is an impartial God. He loves both the wicked and the good children of his at the same level. Even though the wicked committed sins against God, his love knows no reservation for them. That means God's love is really wonderful. We cannot imagine his love because of our sinful minds.

The Creator of everything continues to care for the well being of all his created things. He always has the desire to restore the fallen humanity to their original or perfect state. Therefore, he has done the work of the Saviour of the world too through Jesus Christ. To achieve this task, or so to say, as a part of his works, he became the Saviour of the world through Jesus Christ. He is the Saviour of the world, not only from the New Testament period, but even from the beginning. As Saviour of the world, he has the care and love for every creature of his. Due to his love, God cannot hate human beings even when they are sinful. God's love is not like human love. While the best human beings love only those who love them, God loves sinners too. It is a lovely saying about God, that he hates sin but loves sinners. So, no one ever become God's enemies. Due to his love, God always wants to save sinners from their sins, rather than attempting to destroy the wicked. God always waited for the forgiveness of repented sinners.

Therefore, it is unthinkable for God to hate gentiles and thus fought war for Israel against other nations. God always wants to save sinners from their sins, and thus it is impossible to think of God at war with other nations. God loves both the righteous and sinners at the same level, and Jews and Gentiles too at the same level. So, to say that God initiated war for Israel against other nations is one's own claim. It is one wrong claim on God's attitude to war and killing. To have such a claim shows that human writers are only self-claimers or wrong claimers.

18

God is the God of all Nations

In liberation theologies, God is often designated as "God of the poor", "God of the Dalits", "God of the tribals", etc. These are not taken as absolutization of the designations. Therefore, it also means as follows: "God is God of all, and so he is the God of the poor also", "the God of Dalits too", "the God of the tribals, too", etc. On the other hand, it also means when there is no caste system, dalits may no more be dalits, because, dalitness is or was produced by caste system. When dalits are liberated from dalitness as a result of elimination of caste system, the people who are called dalits, no more need to remain as dalits. Because, such elimination of caste practice, must make present dalits equal with Brahmins and other castes. At such a state dalits would no more be dalits. Because the "word" dalit refers to those who are oppressed, exploited or down trodden, etc.

Therefore, the application of the term to a particular people may be temporal, and not permanent. It is used to describe the people from the situation of their oppression. So, when or if, this situation be removed, the term may no more be applicable to them. Therefore, the designation of God as the God of the Dalits", is a liberative designation of the God of all people. Therefore, it is not confusing to us. The designation is not in an absolute sense. I hope, liberation theologians understood this.

It is the same with the designation of God as the God of tribals", "the God of the poor", etc. Tribalism may or may not be temporal. Almost the same is with poverty. If the terms may be temporal, the designations too must be temporal. If and when "tribalism" and poverty would one day have an end, the designations "The God of the tribals" and "the God of the poor" too may no more be relevant. They are used now as liberative terms.

Israelites' use of the designation, "*Yahweh* is the God of Israel", on the other hand, is used by the Israelites as if it is in an absolute sense. It somehow means that *Yahweh* is the God of Israel alone. It may connote *henotheism* in its application. It means that while other nations worshipped other gods, Israelites are especially set apart for *Yahweh*. It means that Israelites chose God out of many other gods. If it is taken to connote *monotheism*, it must mean that Israelites alone worshipped the true God *Yahweh*. According to this view, *Yahweh* is the true God and Israelites chose the right God. Therefore, Israelites' use of the designations "Yahweh is the God of Israel", or "Yahweh is the holy one of Israel", do not have the same connotation with the designations "the God of the poor", "the God of the tribals". Therefore, we may say that although one can call God as "God of Dalits too", and the God of the tribals too", it is wrong to designate him as God of Israel in the sense that he is the God of Israel alone.

The New Testament is able to show us the fact that God is the God of all nations. The New Testament shows us God's love and concern for the salvation not only of Jews, but also of Gentiles. It is wrong to claim that God is the God of a particular nation. It is wrong to claim that God is the God of Israelites alone. God is the God of all nations.

The Book of Jonah rightly described the wrong Israelites' view of God loving Israelites alone. The book shows that Israelites were selfish to share the good tidings to gentiles. The book also shows, on the other hand, that God loves gentiles too. He sent Jonah to preach the good news to the Gentiles in the city of Nineveh. This shows that God is the God of Gentiles too. As much as God is the God of Israelites he is also the God of Gentiles. He loves both Jews and Gentiles. Therefore, it is not only wrong, but even sinful, to claim that God participated in Israelites' war with other nations. Although, God is worshipped in different religions in different names and different ways, he is one and only one. He is the God of all nations. This is made clear in the next chapter.

19

God is One

The Old Testament shows us the fact that ancient Israelites oscillated between ***monotheism*** and ***polytheism*** and between ***monotheism*** and ***henotheism***. While pure Judaism tried to maintain pure ***monotheism***, the people often got astrayed from such teachings of Judaism. Prophets really taught ***monotheism***. They used to claim that ***Yahweh*** alone is God, and other gods are not gods, they are idols only. Prophet Isaiah claims that other gods worshipped in the forms of idol are not gods. They are dead idols only.

However, there also existed belief in ***polytheism*** among the ancient Israelites. They often chose to worship idols. When Moses returned late from a base on Mount Sinai, Israelites made a golden calf and tried to worship it. This seemed to show that Israelites often recognized presence of other gods too under the leadership of Aaron. Israelites showed that there is possibility of worshipping other gods too. *Polytheism* is a possible part of the content of the mind of an Israelite in ancient Israel.

There is also an idea of ***henotheism*** in the Old Testament. Israelites have the view that they chose ***Yahweh*** out of many gods, or ***Yahweh*** had chosen Israelites for himself. Thus, Israelites are supposed to worship Yahweh alone out of other gods.

It is probably true to say that Israelites believed war and waged war as a result of this wrong belief in presence of other gods. According to this belief, each nation had its own God. War, between nations were thus, believed to be wars between Gods. Therefore, it may be possible to convince Israelites that war is wrong, if we are able to convince them that God is one, or that there is only one God. Almost everyone can now know the fact that there cannot be more than one God. Almost everyone can agree with the fact that God is one. Since God is one, it is totally wrong to say with ancient Israelites, that, war between two nations is war between two gods.

It is necessary here to convincingly state that God is one, and that beliefs in **polytheism** and **henotheism** are wrong views based on ignorance. In order to convince Christians and non-Christians, that God is one, we need to clarify some problems.

19.1. Solution to the Problem of Gods of the Nations

In the ancient world each nation was believed to have its own god. Some nations might have two or more gods. Accordingly war between two nations would often be regarded as war between two gods. Victory of one nation over another nation would also be taken as victory of one god of the nation over the god of the defeated nation. Therefore war must have been accepted as God's action too. Wars must have been fought with the view that gods permitted them to do so.

However, it is realized today that God is one and every nation worshipped the same God in their own ways. People of each religion understood the truth according to their dreams, visions, philosophy, etc. Dreams visions, revelations, may guide, or misguide dreamers, visioners, etc. according to each person's beliefs. They used to think that God spoke to them through dreams, visions, and revelations. However, since dreams and visions are not infallible means of God's revelation, each man's/woman's view of God and his revelations are different from one person to another. So, scriptures show us that there are so many differing views on God.

We are sure now that different views about God in different religions or different nations are not proofs for presence of different gods, but are proofs for presence of different human views of the one God according to differences in dreams, visions, etc. of different people in different religions. God is one, people of different religions understood him in different ways, because, the knowledge they have did not come directly from God. So, they are different from each other.

Different names for God in different religions are human made names for God, so there are so many names for God in the world. If there is only one name for God in the world in the past and at present, it would more easily tempt us to accept to know God's name. However, presence of so many names for God in the world helps us realize the fact that there is no human being who really knows the name of God.

19.2. Claims for Works of God in Different Religions

In the ancient world each nation claimed to have different gods with different names. They used to claim that their own gods used to work this way and that way. Greeks used to claim that their god had a specific way of work, which may be different from Jewish claim for *Yahweh's* works. Romans claimed that their god works specifically. This may be different from Philistines' claim for the work of their own god.

How can we reconcile these views with our claim that God is one and that he works only in one way or one principle of work? One or both of the following points may be accepted as true.

(a) While God is one, he works in many different ways. Different people see different parts of the works of God. For example, Hindus see one part of God's work, and failed to see other parts of God's works. Christians may see some parts of God's works, and failed to see other parts of the works of God. In the same way, Muslims may see some parts of God's works but failed to see other parts of God's works. Accordingly, we are able to see the fact that different ways of understanding God's works in different religions are only different ways of understanding parts of the works of one and the same God. These different understandings of different works of God does not prove presence of many gods in the universe. They are only understandings of different parts of works of one and the same God.

(b) Another way of understanding this is that God is one and human beings have their own ways of understanding works of God. Since some of these understandings are wrong, they have differences.

While God is one, and works consistently, human beings understand his works in their own ways. Thus, presence of opposing views or different views of works of God is not proofs for the existence of many Gods, but are proofs for failure of human beings to know God's works as they really are. God is one and his oneness should not be confused due to presence of so many differing views.

19.3. Paul's View of the Unknown God Proves Oneness of God

Once Paul visited the city of Athens. Once he stood at the centre of the Areopagus and said to the Athenians that they were very religious in all things. Because, in their former worship, they had an inscription" "To an unknown God", on an altar. According to Paul, the people of Athens at that place were very religious, even in their own primal religion. That means, he accepted the religiosity of people in other religions, or primal religions. Paul also told them that the God they have worshipped unknowingly was/is the Father of Jesus Christ. This means that although those people were not Christians in our own sense of the term, the God they had worshipped at that time, at that particular place, was/is one and the same God with the Christian God. Because, God is one or that there is only one God, and although people of different religions worshipped God in their own ways, or knowledges, they all are worshipping one and the same God. This shows that God is one and worshippers worshipped him in different ways. Although, they may not agree to each other, worshippers worshipped one and the same God in their own understood ways.

19.4. John's Way of Referring to the Logos as the Messiah

Logos was the God of the Greeks, and gentiles. For them the Logos was the one through whom, in whom and by whom everything was created. He is the Light of the world.

John uses this term to talk about the Messiah to the Greeks. This means that, to John, the Creator God of the Greeks called the Logos, was no other than the Messiah of the Jews. This means that without the knowledge of the Greeks, their own Creator God was one and the same with the Messiah of the Jews. In the same way

Indian theologians claimed that Avatar of Hindus is the incarnated one of the New Testament.

This shows us the fact that, according to John, people of different nations and religions worshipped one and the same God, under different names for God, and in different forms of worship.

Both, Paul and John would agree that God is one and he is understood and worshipped in different names and in different ways. Although, worshippers may not reconcile to each other or may not even realize that they are worshiping one and the same God, they all looked at one and the same God while worshipping God.

Now, true knowledge of the one God must be a means to realize the evil of war between two nations. It must be especially true for Israelites who still hold that they are especially chosen by God and that Yahweh is their God alone, while other gods are worshipped by other nations. Those who realize the fact that God is one and those who worship God in one way or the other, worshipped the same God, must realize the fact that war between nations is an evil against the will of God.

Isaiah and Jeremiah really talked of a kind of knowledge through the Messiah in the New covenant. This kind of new knowledge of God is supposed to change human beings' attitude to each other. True knowledge of the one God must be a means to have peace in the world. This shows that although people of different religions worshipped God in different ways and in or under different names, they are worshipping one and the same God in different ways in different names.

20

God is the God of Peace

Many writers of the Old Testament wrongly pictured God as the God of war,-warrior, and captain of the army, one who initiates war between Israelites and other nations, and one who fought for Israel against other nations. This idea of picturing God as the God of war, seems to be an accepted idea in ancient Israel. If this teaching is an accepted view in Judaism, Judaism must have been taken as founded on human knowledge of God.

However, there are enough passages in the Old Testament which supported the view that God is the God of peace. To the writer of the book of Judges "*Yahweh* is the Lord of peace."[28] Although Gideon too fought war with other nations, he built an altar to "*Yahweh Shalom*". Prophet Isaiah shows the fact that God who rules in heaven and can create peace.[29] If God is Lord of peace who can create peace, he can never be warrior, nor" captain of the army". It is true to say that the title "Lord of peace" ("*Yahweh Shalom*") is a title given to God by human beings. It is a right giving of a title for God. Since this title is true for God, the opposite titles "Warrior", "captain of the army", etc. must be taken as wrong titles made for God. According to the writer of the Book of Job,[30] God causes peace in the high places. Although, there could not be peace on earth due to human sinfulness, God makes peace in the high places. Wherever there is obedience to God, there is peace. This means that, God always love peace. It is only human beings who destroyed peace. It is only human beings who destroyed peace processes. It is sinful Israelites who claimed that God fought for Israelites.

Prophet Isaiah[31] talks of the Davidic king who would be borne in future as "Prince of Peace". This "Prince of Peace" is believed in future to be the son of God, who in theological term is re-designated by many as "God the Son". If he is the "Prince of Peace" God must be "the King of Peace". Accordingly God is the Lord of Peace rather than the God of war who fought for Israel. Although, the terms "King" and "Prince" become outdated terms, one could see from ancient use of the terms for God and the Messiah, the idea of the Lord of peace rather than the God of war. To any modern reader the designation "Lord of Peace" appears to be more appropriate for God than "God of war".

It is "the Lord of Peace" who longs for eschatological and complete peace between human beings and animals, and between animals and animals,[32] and even between human beings and human beings. Anyone can agree with the truth that God wants complete peace between all living beings.

Even the work of peace through the life and teachings of Jesus are done according to the will of the God of peace. Jesus was commissioned to do the will of God. One or the main part of his mission was to bring forth peace in the world. To achieve perfect peace in the world must be the possible result of salvation of the whole creation. This is the will of the God of peace who wants the work of peace. As much as the God of peace wants the work of peace to be achieved through Jesus Christ, he wants Christians to fully achieve peace in the world. Lasting peace cannot be achieved by threatening with nuclear bombs, with the power of superiority.

Endnotes

28. Cf. Judges 6:24.
29. Isaiah 45:7.
30. Job 25:2.
31. Isaiah 9:6.
32. Isaiah 11:1-9.

21

God is the Non-Resistant God

Although, some writers of the Old Testament not only talked of God as a resistant God, but even talked of Him as a revengeful God, angry God, and even as warrior, captain of the army of Israel, we could see the true nature of God as a non-resistant and even an open God through the life of the one who says, "He who has seen me has seen the Father."

Before describing God as the non-resistant God, let us have a brief note on the Old Testament view of God as the angry, wrathful, revengeful and impatient God, and even as warrior or captain of the army of Israel. The Old Testament writers often pictured God as the angry God or revengeful God. He is said to punish sinners instantly or immediately after the people committed sin. The writer of the book of Exodus claimed that God punished the Egyptians by killing their firstborn sons. Some writers also claimed that God used to punish Israelites when they became wicked against God. God sent snakes to bite and kill Israelites for their disobedience and wickedness. Sometimes God used fire, earthquake, to punish the wicked. Israelites were taken captives by Assyrians around 721/2 BC, due to their sins against God (cf. II Kings 17:5-23). The city of Jerusalem was taken and the people were deported to Babylon as captives (cf. II Kings 25:1-22). The cause of this misfortune is claimed to be the people's sin. The work of deportation took place in 597 BC and 587/6 BC. This way of interpreting misfortunes or events in human history may be the works of fatalists who regarded human history to be totally controlled by God. God is often pictured too as angry God who cannot easily be approached by human beings. Anyone who sees God's face must die. God cannot be approached. God is also often pictured as the God of war. He is a "warrior", who is fighting for Israel. (Cf. Exodus 15:1-18; Deuteronomy 4:34); or even captain of the army of Israel. So, often, Israelites' war with other nations was taken as "wars of ***YHWH***". Israelites often asked God if they would be allowed to fight with certain nations. So, according to some writers of the Old Testament God is the angry God, who often takes revenge or punishes wicked people immediately or instantly after they would have commited sin. God is a warrior, who used to fight for Israel. However, the Old Testament alone too have enough response to this view. The Book of Job claims that even righteous people used to suffer. It tries to prove that sufferings are not always resulted by sin. Some sufferers could be righteous people. The book tries to disprove the Jewish view that sufferings are always because of sin.

Through Jesus we could realize that God is the non-resistant God, the God of love, who is also a longsuffering and forgiving God. God is often seen to be inactive, because, he does not even resist evil against Him. As Christians we trust Paul to describe Jesus more correctly than any other writers of the New Testament. Paul says that Jesus is the image of the invisible God. If we believe this view of Paul, we must also agree that we must somehow be able to know God through Jesus Christ. Once some people said to Jesus, "show us the Father". The answer of Jesus is "He who has seen me has seen the Father". This and Paul's view of Jesus Christ as "the image of the invisible God" suggested that Jesus is the self-revelation of God and through Him and by Him we can know and see God. The words of Jesus here may not refer to the physical likeness of Jesus Christ to the Father. It may refer to moral or spiritual likeness of the Son to the Father. Athanasius claimed that the Son Jesus Christ is of the same substance with the Father. Jesus once said to the disciples, "I and the Father are one". (John 2). However, all these do not refer to the identity of the Son and the Father. Although, they are one, they are not identical. It is wrong to say that the Son is the Father, and the Father is the Son.

Our intention is to say that although they are not identical, they are one in some respects. And therefore, we can learn/know about God through Jesus. Because, He is the self revelation of God. What we learn through Jesus Christ is, not only non-violence, but also non resistance. This means that Jesus is a non-violent, non-resistant being. If and since He is a non-violent, non-resistant being, we learn that God is a non-violent, non-resistant God. In another chapter we say that Jesus taught non-violence, non-resistance. He lived a non-violent life. His death on the cross shows His non-violence, His non-resistance. The cross is the zenith of His move for non-violence and non-resistance. Thus, through Him we see God as a non-violent, non-resistant God. It may be useful to repeat the teachings, life and works of Jesus through which we have learn non-violence and non-resistance. Once Jesus said, "Do not resist an evil doer. But if anyone strikes you on the right cheek, turn (to him/her) the other also... (Matthew 5:39). The first part of this quotation may be taken to talk of non-violence, while the latter part may be taken to refer to non-resistance. To Jesus non-resistance is not only necessary but is even useful as a means to spread the Gospel. The Gospel is believed to be spread more successfully through non-violence and non-resistance. Jesus also taught his disciples not to hate but to love enemies. It is impossible for people who are self-centred to love enemies. However, it may not only be possible but even easy to love enemies for those who are selfless. Non-violence and non-resistance are also seen in and through the life of Jesus Christ. Just after the prayer of Jesus at Gethsemane, he was arrested by his enemies. Peter tried to protect or defend Jesus and cut off one ear of Malchus (John 18;10). Instead of supporting or saying thanks to Peter he scolded and asked him to put his sword into its sheath (Jn. 18:6-11). Thus, he allowed Himself to be arrested, persecuted, tortured and even to be crucified. This is more than non-violence, and is non-resistance. Due to His non-violence and non-resistance he faced death on the cross. Thus, we see non-violence and non-resistance through the teachings, works and life of Jesus Christ.

As has already been said Jesus is the image of the invisible God in Paul's theology. If this is true, we can see what God is through the teachings, works and the life of Jesus Christ. In the same way the words of Jesus “I and the Father are One” and” he who has seen me has seen the Father” told us that the non-violence and non-resistance of Jesus show us that God is the non-violent and non-resistant God. Since no one can see God, one possible way to claim that God is a non-violent, non-resistant God is, through the theology of Paul and through the teachings, works and life of Jesus Christ. Human history and history of Christianity showed that God hardly or never punish any sinner instantly or immediately. As much as he never protected his early Christians from persecution and other sufferings, He never or hardly punish sinners instantly or immediately. Early Christians were thrown into the dens of lion, burn on the stakes, killed in numbers by the Roman soldiers. God at such a time seems to remain silent, non-violent or non-resistant. He never (or hardly) punish persecutors, terrorists, adulterers, fornicators, war-lovers, murderers, etc. who committed sin against God himself. So, we see God as non-violent, non-resistant God who never involved Himself in war, one who never punish any sinner instantly or immediately.

Such God can never allow war between His children. Since all are His children God must never allow war between His children. Since He is the non-violent God, non-resistant God, no one can suspect God to be a lover of war, or warrior. Since the true God is the non-violent, non-resistant God, any God who is described as violent or war-loving God or warrior God is an idol god, because, he is not the true God. Another way of putting it is to say that the true God may be described wrongly. He may be described as warrior, captain of the army, a guide in war, a commander in war, etc. To describe God this way is to idolize him. It is to describe God as wicked God, wicked like one of the Israelites. It is better to call God as a drunkard God than to call him warrior, captain of the army or God of war. Because, as is shown in another chapter, war is possibly the greatest sin in human history as it is the most destructive sin. Therefore, to call God as God of war or warrior or captain of army of Israel, is to take Him or worship Him as the most sinful being. Therefore, it is best to avoid use of these terms for this God of love.

For anyone who accepted the divinity of Jesus Christ it is right to see God’s non-violence, non-resistance through the teachings, works and life of Jesus. Because, He is believed to be the self-revelation of God. Thus, we are able to say that through His teachings, His works, His life, Jesus is able to proclaim the Good News that God is a non-violent, non-resistant God. Since He is such a God, war and violence cannot have a place in His life. In a sense Jesus Christ did not imitate God's life. He lived God's life. The life he lived is/was God's life. Therefore, His non-violence and His non-resistance could really show us God's non-violence and God's non-resistance.

It is even possible for those who regarded Jesus Christ merely as a human being, who attained God's way of life, to say that we could know what God is, through him. For such Christians who take Jesus merely as human being, attempting to attain divine character in his life, it is not impossible to talk of God's non-violence and non-resistance through him. In this sense Jesus could be understood as mere human being, but different from other human beings in that He did not fall into sin and that He is more like God. Even for such Christians who have this view, the non-violence and non-resistance of Jesus Christ could still show God's non-violence and His non-resistance. Semi-Arians who opposed the divinity of Jesus, still accepted His likeness to the Father.[33] For them too-it is not impossible to accept the view that the non-violence and non-resistance of Jesus could show the non-violent and non-resistant nature of God.

There are signs of estrangement from the truth in every religion. In Hinduism too there is belief in God of war called *Indra. Indra* is a God of war or warrior.[34] This should be taken as a diversion from the truth of God in Hinduism. Both the Jewish belief in God as warrior and Hindu belief in the presence of a God of war called ***Indra*** should be equally condemned as an estrangement from the truth about God. Even if we could allow God to have a time of anger He should never be understood as angry God, God of war, captain of the army, etc. Let God be God, let God be the good God, and let Him be God of love, but not the God of war. To say that God is the God of war is one case of sinful human beings made God in their own images. Human beings are warriors, lovers of war, who think that war is unavoidable in the world. So, to say the same to God is to describe God exactly as sinful human beings. In the same way as a man/woman use to see his/her own face in the mirror, a writer sees himself in his description of God. It may be due mainly to God's invisibility that human beings are not able to describe God as He really is. Since God is invisible human reasoning could not focus on the unseen, but rather on the seen and the human. This led human view of God to focus on the seen and the human, and therefore God is made human in human descriptions of Him.

It is nothing wrong to describe God as human or in human terms, probably because God too is personal and even human in certain sense. However, the danger is in sinful human beings describing God as human. Because, sinful human beings cannot avoid describing God as a sinner. It is in such a situation that God is described as warrior, captain of the army, etc. Therefore, we should now have our eyes open to reject the idea of God as warrior, captain of the army of Israel, etc. And accept the truth that God is, rather, a non-violent, non-resistant God. Such a God cannot accept war as truth. The true God can never accept war as natural in human life.

Endnotes

33. Louis Berkhof, *History of Christian Doctrines,* Edinburgh, 1937, p. 88.
34. Gavin Flood, *An Introduction to Hinduism*, New Delhi, 1998, p. 46.

22

God is Parent of All

One possible way to realize the fact that God cannot and should not initiate war between nations is to realize the fact that God is Parent (Father/Mother) of all human beings. The term used in the Bible is "Father". He is addressed as "Father" for his great care for his children. Jesus compares and contrasts God's love for his children to the love of human fathers. He thought that God's fatherly love is much more than the love of human fathers. Jesus uncritically uses the term "father" for God as there was no such problem at that time. Use of "Father" for God in the Bible may further be explained:

(a) The term "father" was used for God in the Old Testament based on male dominated society. Since writers of the Bible had the mind of male chauvinism, imprinted in their mind, their view of God was male. They could not think of God as female, because they regarded women not only as inferiors, but even as properties. (b) During the time of Jesus, it was not a critical issue. All writers used what was prevalent at that time. Even Jesus was not critical to it. Jesus used it as it was traditional, without any critical mind.

It is feminist theologians who started questioning the use of "Father" for God. They would say that its use is irrelevant for certain reasons as follow. (a) The term "father" for God is one sided. It excluded feminine characteristics of God.

(b) God is spiritual, and so we cannot refer to God as human beings. However, if God is to be described in human terms, inclusive words must be chosen to refer to God. Since the term "father" is not an inclusive term it cannot do justice to God's nature.

It is possible for some feminists to claim that a better word for God in this case is "Mother. Because, a mother's love for her children is the greatest human love. So, God's love could be more like a mother's love than that of a father. Mothers used to feed their children with their own milk (body). They used to carry them from the time of their formation in the womb. They used to care for them as if they care for their own body. So, there is no human love which is greater or higher than a mother's love. Therefore, the best human term to designate God for his love and care for his children is "mother."

However, this too is not the most appropriate word for some reasons (a) It is also a one-sided word. It too excluded maleness. If it is used in place of "Father" for God we may arouse "Male-movement to remove or replace it again. So, it is not a perfect term for the situation. (b) Moreover, even mothers' love cannot equal God's love. God's love is still higher than the love of mothers. So, for these two and other reasons the designation "mother" for God is not a more appropriate term to replace the term "father" for God.

We are forced to accept the feminists' claim for use of either "father and mother" or "parent" to replace the term "Father" for God.[35] Since either of them conveys similar meaning, they are used interchangeably. Accordingly, God is our "Father and Mother" or "Parent." This chapter is entitled "God is Parent of all". Choice of "Parent" in place of Father instead of "Father and Mother" in this chapter does not have much significance. It only denotes its shorter expression. It is chosen here only because it is shorter than "Father and Mother."

Accordingly, God is Parent of all human beings. God is Parent of all human beings without any exception. All human beings may be convinced that God is Parent of all human beings. Parent of all human beings cannot allow war between his children. God is not wicked Parent. He is a good Parent of all human beings. There is no place for permission of war in him. Even when two children of a father could fight each other, good parents never allow them to fight. God is not a wicked Parent. It is not in his nature to allow war between his two children.

Jesus points out the fact that more than wicked human fathers could do good things to their children, God is able to do more good things for his children. It is not in God's capacity to throw bones between dogs. God would never allow war between nations, or between ethnic groups. It must only be human beings who claimed that God participated in wars at the side of Israelites against other nations. Parent of all human beings can never fight for one group of children in war against other groups. Jesus really shows us the fact that God loves all his children at the same level. He says that God sends rain upon both the good and the wicked. He uses this idea to make clear that God does not especially love any one because of his/her good-nesses. The reasons may be as follow:

(a) God is not a partial God. He has no partiality. He has no partiality for his good children against his wicked children.
(b) This is so because he is not a human being. He is God. One must not think that God has this sin of partiality for one of his children against other children of his.
(c) He loves both the good and the wicked at the same level. Jews must have misunderstood God's love, because of their lack of knowledge. They need to study the love of God all over again, in order to realize the fact that God's love is a mystery to spiritually selfish people. It is a mystery which forgives sinners and accepts them too as his children.
(d) One can also separately say that since God is Parent of all that he treated all human beings equally. He is not a wicked Parent. He is a good and loving Parent. So, he loves all and cares for all.

The parable of the prodigal son may somehow be taken as a correction of the Jewish misunderstanding of God as loving Jews alone but hated gentiles. According to that parable, the father of the two sons loves both the sons, even though the younger son wasted his life in a sinful way. The father of the two sons loves the elder brother who was at home. He also loves the younger son who spent his life in sinful ways. He longed for his return to normal life. When he returned home, he (the father) prepared a big feast for him (the returned son) with costly gifts. The elder son became selfish or has had envy for the love of the father for the younger son too. Here, the father's love could not be fully understood by the elder son. The father loves the younger son as much as he loves him (the elder son). This describes God's love. God loves both the good and the wicked equally. In the same way God, as Parent of all, loves both the Jews and the gentiles. It is impossible to think of God imposing war between Jews and gentile nations. It is totally wrong to claim that God sent Israelites to fight war with Gentiles.

It is acceptable to all Christians, Jews and non-Christians, to say that Parent of all human beings must never allow war between his good and wicked children. It is wrong to say that God would ask Jews to destroy gentiles in war, as much as it is totally wrong for the father of the two sons in that parable, to impose war between the two sons. This loving Parent of all human beings must rather love all equally, without partiality, envy, discrimination, etc.

Endnotes

35. R. L. Hnuni, "Patrirchal Cultures and Traditions in the Bible" in *Feminist Hermeneutics*, IWIT/ISPCK, Delhi, 2002, pp. 82- 84.

23

All Human Beings are Brothers and Sisters

Basing on a Christian view of the universality of sin, we do say that since Jews were born in or under the environment of sin, their eyes were not open enough to see that all human beings are their brothers and sisters. As soon as a Jewish child is grown up, he is taught that other nations are their enemies. It is since the time of the exodus and the conquest of Canaan that young Israelites used to be grown up with the belief that other nations are enemies of both the Israelites and God. Thus, wars were often fought with other nations with the view that they were fighting with enemies, but not with brothers.

It is our mission to convince Israelites/Jews that all human beings are brothers and sisters. A right thinking Jew and Christian and even people of other religions, must agree that all human beings are brothers and sisters. It is true to say that all human beings are brothers and sisters for certain reasons.

(a) Since God is Parent of all, all human beings are brothers and sisters. (b) Since all human beings have common origin, they have blood relationships. They are, thus, brothers and sisters. (c) Since the whole world is one family of human beings, all are brothers and sisters. A brief note on each of these points may be necessary.

(a) Most people may agree that since God is "Parent" of all human beings, all human beings are children of God and, thus, are brothers and sisters. It is not unbiblical to say that God is Parent of all human beings. Anyone who agrees with this view must agree that all human beings are children of God. It is not wrong to say that all children of God must be brothers and sisters.

(b) All Christians do agree that all human beings have common origin. Most of them also agree that all human beings have blood relations. Therefore, it is also true to say that all human beings are brothers and sisters.

Most Christians cannot accept Darwin's theory of evolution[36] through the survival of the fittest. Although, it may not be true to say that the names of the first man and woman were Adam and Eve, it is taken as true to say that God has created the first man and woman to be the parents of all human beings. Through them all human beings have blood relations. Scientists may or may not say that the claim for the blood relationship of all human beings through the first man and woman is wrong because different nations have different blood. If some scientists would understand that those who have different bloods do not have blood relations, they may claim that all human beings do not necessarily come from common or same parents. By knowing or not knowing the fact, Christians may claim that there must be a time or possibility in human history when or where blood differences could be caused by conceptions in women's womb or by any outside or inside processes. We need theological or scientific discovery to finalize this argument. Even though we cannot have any infallible argument on this blood relationship of all human beings, we can have a way of claiming that all human beings are brothers and sisters. We can say that all human beings are brothers and sisters because they all are one kind of God's Creatures.

(c) Since the whole world is one family, they all are brothers and sisters. Today emphasis is made on the whole world as one house, one family, in which all human beings are said to be brothers and sisters.

In a narrow sense, Christians would like to say that this brotherhood/sisterhood should be mentioned only among the Christians. However, in a wider perspective, all human beings are said to be brothers and sisters. We need a kind of realization of all human beings as one family. When God made everything and human beings, there was nothing to destroy the family relationship of all created beings. But when the population of human beings in the world began to increase more and more, sin also became increased. This coincidence of increase of human population and human sin increased the gap between small families, and begot hatred between nations. Gradually, feeling of difference between nations became increased more and more until nations regarded each other as enemies. This in one sense caused hatred between nations. It was not caused by God. In order to restore the original state of human fellowship as one family, sin must be destroyed. This means that salvation of human beings from their sins would also result into restoration of all human beings as one family. An unavoidable result along with this would be the realization that all human beings are brothers and sisters. This means that to restore brotherhood/sisterhood of all human beings is a part of the gospel too.

It must be a part of the message of Prophet Jonah. A part of the good news brought to the people of Nineveh by him seemed to be to bring back brotherhood/sisterhood between the Jews and the people of Nineveh.

The parable of the Prodigal son (of Jesus) may also be taken to convey brotherhood/sisterhood between Jews and gentiles. Whether it was the main purpose of the parable or not one can use the same parable to emphasize brotherhood/sisterhood between Jews and gentiles. The parable may be allegorized to say that the father in the parable was God and the elder son represents the Jewish (Israelite) nation, while the younger son, who wasted his life, represents the gentile world (in the sense only of the Jews). In the sense of the Jews (not in sense of Jesus or God) Jews (or Israelite) never astrayed from God. Gentiles alone astrayed from the way of God. Therefore, the elder son in this parable is fitting for the Jews, and the younger son, who ran away from home and wasted everything, is fitting to symbolize the Jewish view of the gentiles.

However, according to Jesus in the parable, the brotherhood/sisterhood, between the elder brother and the younger brother was broken only in the mind of the elder brother, but not in the mind of the father and in the mind of the younger son. In the same way, the brotherhood/sisterhood between Jews and gentiles is never absent in the sight of God. It was only in the sight of Jews (Israelites) that gentiles are no more real brothers/sisters. Unless Jews regarded

Jesus as enemy, gentiles would still take them as blood brothers. It was Jews/Israelites who first destroy brotherhood/sisterhood with gentiles. According to this parable Jews and gentiles are still brothers and sisters. Both Jews and gentiles need to realize each other that they are brothers/sisters. This realization may be caused by a strong spiritual or physical awakenings.

Jews may also be taught that wicked brothers in any human family continued to be brothers in the family. Even though some wicked children used to commit sins against their parents and brothers or sisters, they are never cut off from the family. In the same way, even though Jews regarded gentiles as sinful people they continued to be children of God and wicked brothers or sisters of Jews.

If Jews and gentiles could be convinced to accept this view, they must be convinced to accept the view that war between brothers is unthinkable for God too. It is unthinkable and wrong to think that God would allow war between brothers and sisters. Jews are brothers and sisters of gentiles. Both groups are children of God. God must never allow war between them. It must have been the childish view of the Jews/Israelites to say that God allow war or God participated in war for Israel against other nations. Even little children today may agree to say that it is even funny to believe God as warrior, captain of the army of Israel. Even if a brother quarrels with his brother or sister he would not be angry forever. He would soon forget it and live happily again with his brothers/sisters. What is wrong is wrong with Israel. Israelites/Jews must be awakened to realize that other nations are their brothers and sisters. They must re-formulate their wrong/past theology and returned to realize the fact that all human beings are their brothers and sisters. As soon as they could be awakened to see God as he really is, they would see him as Father/Mother of all human beings. As soon as they would see him as Parent of all, they would have their eyes open to see that all human beings are their brothers and sisters. As soon as they come to this stage, they must start dis-armament (of weapons).

Endnotes

36. (Charles Darwin, ***Origin of Species,*** 1959), Quoted by Zacharias Mattam, ***Opening The Bible,*** Bangalore, 1988, p. 68, 69.

24

A Prophetic Vision of the Peaceful World in the Future

Some ancient Israelite/Jewish prophets really fore-see a peaceful world in the midst of war and chaos in the world. Prophet Isaiah especially fore-saw a perfect peace which will usher in the future with the restoration of a Davidic king in future. Isaiah talked of the coming of a shoot from the stump of Jesse, and that branch shall grow out of his roots.[37] It "should be taken to mean that Judah, with, its capital at Jerusalem, had already fallen into the hands of Babylon. Judah, at that time, was left only like a tree which had already been cut down. It only remained as a portion of the tree left after it is cut down, i.e. the stump. This means that at that time Judah was left not only like fruitless, but even like a branchless tree. The stump of a tree can no more be called a tree. In the same way, Judah, at that time, was no more a nation. They were left captives in the land of Babylon. Although, the said passage is in the Proto-Isaiah, the meaning of the passage seems to refer to this.

However, the prophet foretold that the fallen dynasty of Judah would be restored to power, with the birth of a Davidic king in future. This Davidic king will rule with righteousness. He shall judge the poor with righteousness. With his rule, the earth shall be full of the knowledge of the Lord, as the waters cover the sea. Because, of this kind of knowledge there will be perfect peace on earth. There would be peace between animals and animals, and between animals and human beings, as a result of this new knowledge of God through the Davidic king.

Christians may have a tendency to say that this perfect peace between all living beings would happen only after the final consummation. This kind of perfect peace between all living beings can happen in the following ways. In some animal sanctuaries even tigers are tamed to play with human beings. In India where Hindus avoid killing of animals, animals do not fear human beings nor do they take human beings as their enemies. In tribal areas of India where animals are killed, animals are much more coward and much more fierce than animals in Hindu heart lands in India. This fact partly (or fully) proves that animals could be friends to themselves as well as friends of human beings if human beings were not wicked against them, i.e., if human beings totally avoid killing of animals from the very beginning.

As Christians, our eyes are open wider to see Genesis 1 in which the writer seems to say that animals (everything) are made for food for human beings. However, our eyes are closed not to see other passages which emphasize vegetarianism as more spiritual in the book of Daniel, importance of perfect peace between animals and animals and human beings in Isaiah (quoted above), the need for the redemption of animals in Romans 8, importance of peace between all creatures in heaven and on earth. This means that even our readings of the Bible is overpowered by selfishness, gluttony, one sidedness, etc.

If there would be a good and right reading of the Bible among Christians, and Jews, the following would have happened.

(a) A reading of Deuteronomy[38] would convince Christians to preserve animals by sparing the lives of mother birds. It must be regarded as a means to live long on earth.

(b) A reading of the Book of Daniel[39] must convince a much more spiritual and mature Christians to become vegetarians. If followers of the ways of Daniel would increase in number among the Christians, number of vegetarians must have increased among the Christians.

(c) A right reading and application of Isaiah's message (quoted above) in Christian life would gradually cause perfect peace between animals and animals and between animals and human beings.

(d) A right reading of Romans[40] would cause greater concern for the redemption of animals and the whole creation and this right readings must be a means to bring perfect peace in the world.

According to prophet Isaiah perfect peace must be a achieved in the following ways.

(a) The coming of the Messiah, that Davidic king, will give perfect knowledge of God to the true believers of God.

(b) This new and revealed knowledge will melt the lives of true believers. They will love God's creation as a reflection of their love for God. This means that those who really know God must love God and thus love his creation too.

(c) Due to this knowledge of God, believers must realize the fact that the whole creation is the relatives and neighbours of human beings. This new knowledge of God will provide believers with new way of looking at all human beings as relatives and closed neighbours. This new attitude must totally do away with all hatreds and wars. Therefore, the coming of the Messiah, that Davidic king, must cause perfect peace between all living beings. This perfect peace is believed to be twofold. One would be peace between human beings and animals and the second would be peace between animals and animals.

The fulfillment of this perfect peace is understood in three ways. Jews may say that since the Messiah has not yet come this message of perfect peace cannot happen now. This peace will happen only when the Messiah would come in future. Many Christian commentators may say that although the Messiah has already come in the person of Jesus, this perfect peace will happen only after his second coming. This is inevitable for many Christians, because since we believed that writer of Genesis says that God made animals to be food for human beings, there cannot be peace between God's creatures until we stop killing animals and eating meat.

Many Hindus may claim that Isaiah's vision of perfect peace have already happened among lovers of animals. In Hindu areas animals are not afraid of human beings. Because, many Hindus do not kill animals. Since many Hindus have peaceful minds towards animals, animals in their areas are different from animals in Christian areas. Animals in Hindu areas are much more peaceful than animals in Christian areas. A Hindu may say that perfect peace predicted by Isaiah may happen among human beings at present, if human beings totally stop killing of animals and totally stop eating of meat of wild animals.

Ecologists too may claim that the vision of perfect peace of prophet Isaiah need to be actualized by Christians as a result of deeper knowledge of God through that Davidic king. Those who have deeper knowledge of God through Jesus Christ must also love God. Those who love God must love his creatures as a reflection of their love for God. At the same time such believers would see God's creatures as friends, but not as objects of games. They can have eyes of love.

Ecologists, would claim that a deeper knowledge of God also include actualization of such love of animals into practice. Love in practice is real love for I John.[41] Until there is love, there seems no true knowledge of God. When human beings really love animals and trees, there can be real peace on earth. Real peace in the world must be the result of deeper or real knowledge of God through Jesus Christ, actualized in practice. If Christians can be those who can actualize God's promise in their daily lives, Isaiah's vision of perfect peace may happen in their own generations.

The practical actualization of Isaiah's vision of perfect peace can happen only in the lives of those who put love into practice. Isaiah's vision of perfect peace could happen in the lives of Christians today, only if they stop killing animals and stop eating meat of wild animals. Disorderliness or chaos is caused in the world by human beings' sinfulness against animals and trees. So, to restore perfect peace in the world would be possible only when sins against animals and trees, etc., be totally stopped/abandoned.

Isaiah's vision of perfect peace in the world, seems to include the view that in order to have perfect peace between human beings, there is the need of peace between human beings and animals and between animals and animals. Peace between human beings and animals must be in coincidence with peace between animals and animals. Since enmity and hatred between human beings and human beings, and between human beings and animals, and between animals and animals is caused by human sinfulness, perfect peace can be restored in the world only by eliminating sin in the world.

It is believed that prophet Isaiah saw the vision of perfect peace as the will of God. Even a child would choose perfect peace as the will of God rather than choose war as the will of God. If and since perfect peace is the will of God, he may never join war between Israelites and gentiles. Since perfect peace is the will of God one can infer without mistake that it was not God who used to participate in war between Israelites and gentiles. Rather, it must be the view of ignorant Israelites who thought that God used to support Israelites in their war with other nations.

Endnotes

37. Isaiah 11:1-9.
38. Deuteronomy 22:6-7.
39. Daniel 1.
40. Romans 8:19-23.
41. 1 John 3:16-18

25

The Place of War in the List of Sins

It may not be the interest of theologians to divide smaller and greater sins. It is also difficult to divide smaller sins and greater sins. However, let us use this chapter to try to point out the place of war in the list of sins committed against God. There are sins which do not harm others and sins which badly harm others. Accordingly, one may locate the place of war in list of sins, by looking at its bad effects against people.

(a) Harmless Sins

There are some sins which appeared to be harmless for others. Such sins which do not harm others may somehow be regarded as smaller sins. There is difficulty in pointing out harmless sins to others. One can hardly point out whether sinful thoughts in the mind can harm others or not. Sinful thoughts such as envy, selfishness, pride, etc. may remain harmless to others if they are kept in control. These sins are supposed to be controllable until one may fall into sin. However, they were included in the list of the seven deadly sins of the early Church.[42] Therefore, one may not be willing to accept them among the smaller sins.

Some one may claim that some drunkards used to drink without harming others. However, they are also supposed to cause so many bad effects, such as physical, mental, social, and even spiritual effects. Some drug addicts too could do so without harming others. However, most drug addicts cause many bad effects in the society.

Many of them used to kill themselves within few years. Others who take drugs carefully do so without harming others. Is drug taking a smaller sin for them? The answer is yes and no. Yes because such addicts do harmlessly both against their own body and against others. No, because, drugs used to cause many problems in the world. Some users of alcohol too do so carefully that they do not harm anyone.

Another group of possible harmless sins may include anger without sin, lustful looking of man/woman without practice, covetousness without fulfillment, etc. Someone may say that pride, envy, selfishness, etc. may be kept under control, even to keep them harmless to others.

(b) Harmful Sins

Some sins are much more harmful to others than some sins. For example, murder is not only to make some one loss his/her properties. It is to end the life of another man/woman. It is harmful not only for the victim, but also for relatives or members of the same family. If the victim would be a very important person in a community, killing of such a person would be a great harm to a small community, it would be a great harm to a small community or to a country, etc.

War may often be much more harmful to others than murder. Thousands and millions of people used to be killed in wars. Such lost of life, is caused by so many wars in the world. Wars not only caused lost of countless lives, they also caused lost of properties which worth countless. So, war may top the list of all sins in the world. Trafficking of woman too may be one of the gravest sins, next to rape of women. Persecution of a group of people due to religious causes too must be taken as a grave sin. Fornication and adultery too are grave sins as they are means to pollute the society. Kidnapping of children must be taken as much greater sin than kidnapping of officers. Kidnapping of any human beings should also be at the top as it use to cause fear, sorrow, anger, retaliation, moral depression, etc. To have a correct list of sins from the greatest to the smallest, we may do so by looking at a sin's harmfulness to others.

Sl. No.	Sins
1	War
2	Murder
3	Killing after rape
4	Trafficking of children/women
5	idol worship
6	Rape of women
7	Jhumming/Deforestation
8	Prostitution
9	Tyranny/Colonialism
10	Stealing/Extortion
11	injustice
12	Downtroddenness/Oppression
13	Exploitation
14	defaming others
15	Discrimination/Marginalization
16	Caste Practice
17	Bribery/Corruption
18	Killing of Animals
19	Adultery/Fornication
20	Encroachment
21	Telling Lie/Cheating
22	making fake currency
23	Making Propaganda
24	Drug addiction/Alcoholism
25	Polluting the air
26	Unfair means
27	plagiarism
28	Wrong witness
29	Envy
30	Selfishness/Partiality
31	Pride/anger
32	Self Praise
33	colonialism
34	Coveteousness
35	Laziness/Waste of time
36	Gluttony
37	Changing date of birth

According to this list, war is at the top. Because its harm to human beings is the greatest. It made the greatest effects to human beings. The order of the list may not be the correct list. It may even be a misleading list. However, the list is made to show the fact that war is the most destructive sin in the world. Everyone may agree that war is the most destructive sin.

We are now convinced that God of righteousness can never decide to involve himself in war between Israel and other nations. Because, war is the most destructive sin, and so God may not want to become the most sinful being, by involving himself in committing the sin of warring. Even children can agree to say that God must not like to involve himself in committing the greatest sin. The purpose of this section is to show the fact that war is the greatest of human sins, because, it is the most destructive sin. It is an evil in itself, and is a great sin because of its bad effects. Every religious man/women must agree that God must not agree to involve himself in committing the greatest sin. Every one now can say that God cannot fight war which is one of the gravest of human sins.

Endnotes

42. Car Maninger, *Whatever Became* of Sin, 1995, p.134.

26

A Re-Examination of Israel's Election

It is nothing wrong to accept the view that God has elected Israel in one way or another. However, it is totally wrong to say that God has elected Israel to treat other nations as enemies. So, we need to have a re-examination of the belief in the election of Israel.

Israelite leaders believed that Yahweh has chosen Israel to be special to him. The awareness of God's election is inseparable from the covenant.[43] The account of covenant concluded at Sechem under Joshua makes the history of Israel go back to an election- "I took your father Abraham"... (Jos. 24:3). The election of the people seems to be prepared for by a series of previous election, and it is constantly developed by the choice of individuals newly chosen.[44]

To the patriarchs God shows the continuation of His plan of election. The origin of election is a gratuitous initiative of God: It is Yahweh who "Set this heart on you and chose you" (Deut. 7:7), and not you chose him. The purpose of election is to constitute a holy people, consecrated to Yahweh, "raised above all nations in honour, renown and glory" (Deut. 26:19).

It is no doubt that Israel misunderstood God's choseness. It is true to say that God has chosen the people of Israel to be light to the world, but not to be enemies of the world. It is a wonder that even most spiritual leaders of Israel could misunderstand God's election of Israel as a missionary nation to the world. It probably may not be a special election of Israel as a nation, but only as individuals who especially were chosen by God.

Israel misunderstood God's election as an election of Israel as a nation, to stand against other nations. Israel totally misunderstood God's chosenness only to regard it as a means to hate other nations. It is probably true to say that it is due to its misunderstanding of its chosenness that Israelites believed in war as a means to deal with other nations. In other words, Israel accepted war as a means to deal with other nations, because it misunderstood God's election. Therefore, we are very sure, that, by correcting Israelites' view of its election, we may be able to correct Israel's view of war as a means to deal with other nations.

A correct understanding of God's election of Israel must be a means to reject the idea of war between Israelites and other nations. There is no place at all for war with other nations in the economy of God's election of Israel. We rather surprise as to how a chosen nation would have chosen war as a means to deal with other nations. We may rather doubt that chosenness. We may rather doubt the chosenness of the people of Israel. It may be considerable if other nations misunderstood God's will. However, the chosen people failed to understand the will of God. It is even surprising to hear this fact.

Now it is our task here to correctly interpret God's election of Israel. This correction must lead Israel to abandon war and turn to love other nations. If at all, God has really chosen Israel out of other nations, the purpose must only be to love other people, and take them back to God.

According to the way of God, but not according to the ways of human beings, other nations cannot be the objects of war, but rather as the object of love, the object of concern. The Church should understand that Israel was chosen to be a missionary nation (or rather missionaries), to win the world for God (but not for Israel). Israel was chosen to bear fruit for God as fig trees bear fruits. If Israel fails to bear fruit for God, it could be accursed for not being able to bear fruit, like the cursed fig tree. The purpose of God in electing Israel is to be seen in the Book of Jonah, where Jonah was sent to proclaim the good news to the people of Nineveh. God chose Israel to love gentiles, to proclaim the good news to them, to treat them as relatives, brothers and sisters, to take them back to God. However, Israel failed to understand God's election, and rather hated other nations as enemies. The whole purpose of God in electing Israel failed as a result of Israel's mis-understanding of the purpose of its election. Jonah's negative attitude to his calling reflects the exact position of Israel in misunderstanding the purpose of God's election.

In the whole economy of God's election of Israel, there is no place for war with other nations. It is only as a result of their misunderstanding of God's election that Israel, as a nation, began to hate other nations as enemies. It is Israel's misunderstanding to fail to see the purpose of God's election. As a result of this misunderstanding they fought war with other nations, and only remained like a cursed fig tree. Jesus correctly compared the cursed situation of Israel to/with the cursed fig tree which became dried immediately. If Israel now realized this at present and be awakened to see its present disintegration, it must immediately abandon use of arms both for self defense and for attacking other nations. Because, non-violence and non-resistance alone fits the likeness of elected nation (or people). It is even funny enough to see that elected people of God not only fought war with other nations, but even claim that God initiated Israel's war with other nations, that God is warrior, captain of the army, of Israel, etc.

Conclusion

Some writers of the Bible claimed that God allows holy wars. Some even thought that God is warrior. To call God as a warrior God seems to be possible in *polytheism* in which some gods are believed to be warriors, while there is a good God. Sometimes there is a play on God, i.e., he is even put in the place of "Captain of the army" of Israel. A writer may offer a vacant post of captaincy to God in the army of Israel. It seems that this writer has used God as an object of his game. God may not be angry for this. He may rather feel funny for it. However, we feel funny to think that God may not accept this post. God is often believed to involve himself in wars between Israel and other nations. As much as we do not want to call God as a drunkard, he should not be given the post of "Captain of the army" of

Israel, warrior", "Victor" in wars. Although, the designation "Victor" in war seems to be great, God must have hated it, and rejected the offer. For God even the idea of "holy wars" is either funny, and even hateful.

One can rightly claim that Israelites claimed this idea of God's involvement in wars with other nations, as a result of one or all of the following:

(a) One and the main reason for Israel to say that God involved himself in wars between Israel and other nations is its misunderstanding of its election by God. God seems to elect Israel to be a missionary nation to the world. Israel failed to understand this. Israel rather claimed that it is chosen to be special to him. It is chosen to punish wicked nations. Other nations are enemies of Israel as well as enemies of God. War is a means of punishing wicked nations.
(b) Israel must be influenced by ancient religious' view of gods warring with each other. Gods used human beings to fight each other. Gods used to lead their own people in wars. Thus, Yahweh led his people Israel, as captain of the army. Victory of one nation means victory of the God of that victorious nation. Since God is one, this idea became an outdated view.
(c) Another reason for accepting war is that Israelites were ignorant that every worshipper of God worshipped one and the same God, in one way or another.
(d) Israelites failed to understand God as the God of all nations. They understood him as the God of Israel alone. This allows them to fight war with other nations. Since God is God of all nations, war cannot be accepted.
(e) Israelites often understood God as an angry God or revengeful God. Rather, he is God of love who can forgive sins of all sinners. Therefore war is not necessary.
(f) Israelites allow war between them and other nations because they were ignorant of the fact that God is parent of all. Since God is parent of all nations, it is totally wrong to say that God fought war for Israel against other nations.

It may probably be true to say that God never elect any one nation to be special to him. If at all God really choose anyone nation, such a nation must rather be special in the following ways. (a) Such a nation must be specially good to other nations. They will rather be incapable of hating other nations. (b) because they must be a missionary nation to win the world for God. (c) They must treat people of other nations as their own younger brothers and sisters. (d) If gentiles strikes their right cheek, they should turn their left cheek too to them. (e) They should use the golden rule which says, "Do to others what you wish them done to you" as their norm of life. Since Israelites were far away from these things, their claim for God's special election is doubtful.

Endnotes

43. Jacques Guillet, "Election" in *Dictionary of Biblical Theology,* XL Dufour, Bangalore, (ed.), 1967, p. 138.
44. Cf. *Ibid.*

PART-4

CHRISTIANS' PARTICIPATION IN THE MILITARY SERVICE

There was not only a little hesitation in the early Church to join military service, especially in the Roman Empire but early Christians regarded such service as an evil against God. Therefore, for a long time, Christians did not join military service, especially in the Roman Empire.

Christians joined military services today probably due to gradual change in Christian Theology, especially after the reformation in the sixteenth century. This new attitude to military service in the midst of Christians seemed to be made because of different reasons.

27

A Study of Christians' Joining Military Service

Today most Christians have positive attitude to Christians' participation in military service. However, in the early Church, Christians objected to join military service, due, probably to the following reasons. One reason may be that, since the then Roman Government persecuted Christians, the early Church regarded military power as an enemy of the gospel. The government of Rome, at that time, used military power as an instrument to persecute the early Christians. Therefore, Christians at that time understood military power as an enemy of God and the gospel. At that time Christians would think that to join military service, for a Christian, is a great sin. It is to offer oneself as an enemy of the gospel.

The second possible reason for the early Church, to avoid military service, is their imitation of the non-resistant/non-violent means of Jesus in situations of violence. The early Church saw the life and teachings of Jesus, more exemplary, than the lives of the people of the Old Testament. They read the teachings of Jesus as he says, "Do not take revenge", "forgive each other", "If anyone strikes your right check, turn to him your left too[45]"... They saw Jesus scolding Peter for defending him in front of those who came to arrest him in the garden of Gethsemane.[46] Jesus asked Peter to put his sword into its shield. They saw Jesus silent in front of the high priest and Pilate. They saw Jesus bearing the cross as if he has no power to defend himself or resist evil. They saw the Son of God, carrying his own cross in front of his persecutors as if he has no power to resist himself. He submitted himself to die on the cross, as if he has no one to defend him, or protect him. He died a helpless death on the cross. Those who really know who Jesus is, knew him as a non-resistant, a non-violent being. Thus, his earliest disciples must have thought that Christians must stick to the principle of the New Testament. They are followers of Jesus, and imitators of Jesus. Therefore, military services are not a Christian way.

Probably due to both of these reasons, or for one of them, that earliest Christians avoided military service for centuries. However, with the passing of time and with the dawn of the reformation, Christians gradually felt that military service is necessary for Christians too, as a means to defend one's own country, and as a means to earn one's livelihood. Today Christians no more feel the necessity of avoiding military service. They may now feel that since a Christian is both citizen of the kingdom of God and a citizen in the kingdom of the world, he/she also has the right to defend his/her own country as much as he/she has the right to vote. It is probably after the reformation, in the sixteenth century, that Christians more fully accepted military service not only as a possible means of livelihood, but even as a necessary path of Christian life.

Probably another reason, or similar reason as above, is that it must be Israelites' positive attitude to war that encouraged Christians to join military service. Some Old Testament writers told us that God is Lord of host, warrior,[47] and captain of the army, who leads Israelites in war[48] against other nations. Since, Christians read the Bible as the Word of God, they happened to believe that war is a part of the will of God. With these views in mind Christians continue to join military service in most countries of the world. According to my own imagination, fifty percent of all those who work in the government service in the world, are those who joined military services.

Endnotes

45. Matthew 5:38.
46. John 18:10- 11.
47. Exo. 15:1- 18; Deut. 4:3.
48. Joshua 5:13;Jud.5;4:20; Joshua 10:10 - 11.

28

Christian Life and Military Services

Without much thinking or without second thought, many Christians joined military services without any hesitation. Today we have a tendency to condemn military services for Christians for certain reasons.

28.1. The Purpose of Military Service

The purpose of military services may be described under three heads.

(a) To Earn One's Livelihood

The latest purpose of military service is to earn one's livelihood. Many tribals think that those who have government services are rich people. They are believed to be the blessed people....So, without much hesitation, tribal Christians used to join military services as one of the best means of livelihood for tribal families. Since other government services are not easily given to poor tribals, they find it best to join military services without high educational qualifications too.

It is especially important for poor Christians to earn their livelihood in the easiest way they could have. It may even be sinful to prevent them from getting such services. However, it is also necessary to say that Christians should gradually seek other means of livelihood as means to gradually abandon military services. Because, it is finally wrong for Christians to earn their livelihood through an evil means.

Military service is evil because one of its purposes is to kill enemies, to destroy enemies, and even to rule over others.

(b) To Suppress Evil

One hidden purpose of military service is to suppress evil. It is thought that if there would be no militarism in the world evil may gain more ground in the lives of human beings. The whole world know that militarism, at least partly, suppress evil in the world. Some people may even think that without militarism, life on earth may be short lived. More, people may die at the hands of wicked people in the world. Such people would think that life on earth would be impossible without militarism. Thus, militarism is believed even by Christians as necessary power to suppress evil in the world. Due to this view in mind many Christians joined military services without any hesitation.

However, it is our task in theology to state that the task of the Gospel is not only to suppress evil through the agencies of militarism, but try to eliminate evil from the world by changing individuals. The task of the gospel is to change individuals so that they all may hate evil and thus allow sin to be eliminated from the face of the earth. Accordingly, to try to suppress evil by means of military power is not the way of the Gospel, nor is it believed to be fully successful in eliminating evil by that means. Although, Christians are very weak and are not able to check the spread of evil in the world, they are supposed to do away with sin in the world only by convincing individuals to hate and totally abandon sin. Therefore it is wrong for Christians to join military services whose purpose is to try to suppress evil/sin by force.

(c) To Defend One's Own Country and Wage War if Necessary

According to the governments of the world, military service is necessary to defend or protect one's own country from foreign attacks or evil forces within. No country can remain peaceful without military powers. Everyone must agree that no country may survive without military power to defend one's own country. This fact of military services necessitated military personels to promise to wage war and kill people if necessary. Everyone must agree that anyone who joins military services must take pledge to kill enemies when situations necessitated. Unless military personels pledge to kill enemies, they may not be able to join military services. Therefore, it is contrary to Christian life to make a promise to kill someone. Christians are told to love enemies, rather than to kill them. Therefore, it is even wrong for Christians to join military services. According to me, those who chose to join military services chose to be enemies of Jesus. Because, Jesus is a non-violent and non-resistant teacher and Saviour, who wishes his disciples to imitate his examples. Paul also urges Christians to imitate him as he had imitated Jesus.

28.2. The Sinfulness of the Will to Rule Over Others

War is often (if not always) associated with the will to rule over others. Alexander the Great attempted to conquer the whole world and rule over it. Mighty kings used to fight wars as a means to conquer enemies and rule over them. Countries in the west, such as USA, England, France, Portugal, Germany, etc. colonized many countries of Asia in most parts of the eighteenth century till the early Part of the twentieth century. Long after these Asian countries got independence, theologians of Asia realized that this act of colonization of weaker nations is a grave sin. Liberation theologians today realize the fact that the rich ruling over the poor, high castes ruling over low castes, the strong ruling over the weak, men ruling over women, lords ruling over slaves, the educated ruling over the illiterate, is a kind of sin caused as a result of sinful nature of humankind.

Wars not only ended with self defence. It is often fought as a means to rule over other nations or tribes. This made war more sinful. This means that war could be a means to achieve an evil. It is an evil to achieve another evil.

28.3. The Sinfulness of Arms Race

Arms race seems to be a part of modern life. Every country planned to acquire all kinds of modern weapons. A country felt that it is vulnerable to be victims of war if it fails to procure all kinds of sophisticated weapons today. Rifles almost become an outdated gun. Names like Light Machine Gun (LMG), SLR, A.K.47, etc. becomes unavoidable in any government's list of arms. Every country wants to procure or acquire fastest and best war planes. Every country has a will to have best military forces. Moreover, every country desires to be a super power. Today, to become a super power means to have certain numbers of nuclear bombs, or weapons of mass destruction.

No country tries to have all these weapons only for decoration. Every country has the will to have all kinds of modern weapons as a means to destroy others or at least as a means to warn others. The purpose of arms race in the world today is not to do something good. Rather, it has an evil purpose. It is to destroy others. It is to destroy oneself too. Therefore, it is no more advisable for Christians to join military service.

28.4. There is No Place for Nuclear War in Christian Life

Producers and owners of nuclear bombs may or may not yet fully understand the possible bad effects of nuclear wars in future. Production and use of nuclear bombs may always be related to some or all of the following: (1) It is based on enmity between countries. This enmity between nations is a sin in itself. Christians themselves join military services, and thus they too committed the sin of enmity with other nations. If there would be no enmity between nations, there would be no production of nuclear weapons. Christianity can never justify this enmity between nations as a Christian's way of life. (2) The purpose of producing nuclear bombs is "to destroy others/ enemies. The will to destroy others is the outcome of sin itself. There is nothing good in the production and use of nuclear bombs. How can a Christian appreciate such an evil? How can Christians encourage use of such a destructive weapons? There is no Christian teaching which can allow production and use of nuclear weapons. (3) Nuclear weapons are means to destroy the earth. Almost every one today knows that nuclear wars could destroy the earth. A Hydrogen bomb is believed to be a hundred times more powerful and more destructive than atom bombs used in the Second World War to destroy Nagasaki and Hiroshima in Japan. This means that one hydrogen bomb is enough to destroy one of the biggest cities in the world today. Two thousand hydrogen bombs may be enough to destroy the whole surface of the earth.

Due to this, nuclear programme has no place in Christian life. Because, Christians are supposed to do good to all others. Christians are not supposed to plan evil against others. True Christians are supposed to realize the evil of nuclear programmes.

29

Christians Should not Join Military Service

Christians should not join military service if they want to remain faithful to the Lord. Because, (a) the purpose of military service is to kill and to destroy others. (b) War is against the will of God; (c) God never allows War, (d) It is against the non-violent/non-resistant means of Jesus.

29.1. Because the Purpose of Military Service is to Kill and to Destroy Others

Since the purpose of military service includes the plan to kill enemies and to destroy others, it is not so Christian to join military services. A Christian is supposed to do good to others, rather than to harm others. A Christian should rather do as much good as possible to others, even to feed hungry enemies and to give water to one's thirsty enemies. Christians are supposed to love one's enemies. A study shows us the fact that since Christians are supposed to love enemies, there is no place for war and military service in Christian life. No one can love enemies if one is an enemy? How can a Christian love enemies if he/she joins military service. In order to love enemies one must first avoid military service, and try to do good to others.

29.2. Because War is Against the Will of God

God feels pain whenever any of his creatures is killed or destroyed. God is believed to feel pain whenever so many people are killed in war or in communal clashes. Any right thinking human being must agree with this.

Every Christian who has joined military services cannot and never promise that he/she would not fight war even when it is necessary. He/She must promise to kill enemies when war broke out with other nations. This means that in joining military service, Christians hurt the heart of God. While God feels for the well being and long life of all his creatures, people who have joined military service planned to destroy others.

Our study shows that it is not God himself who asked Israelites to fight war with Canaanites, Philistines, Medianites, Syrians, Assyrians, Amalekites, etc. It is the view of the Israelites that God would fight for Israel against other nations. It is their view that God was warrior, captain of the army of Israel, etc. God does not like war. God really hates war. Therefore, Christians who want to seek the will of God should not and must not join military services, as military services aims to fight war when it is necessary.

29.3. Because it is Against the Non-Resistant/Non-Violent Ways of God

Christians should not join military service, because it cannot avoid war at all times. War is violence. Military service itself is a violent means. Military service is a preparation to use violence to promote violence or evil.

Although, God wants the elimination of evil/sin in the world, He did not use violence. He is non-violent, non-resistant God. The non-violent, the non-resistant means of God is seen mainly through the life and teachings of Jesus.

Jesus Christ is believed to be the self-revelation of God. It also means that God revealed himself through Jesus. For Paul Jesus is the image of the invisible God.[49] This means that God is in Jesus the Christ, that through him and in him we can see what and who God is. Jesus too was quoted to say, "He who has seen me has seen the Father."[50] The life and teachings of Jesus show us the will of God. Jesus taught his followers not to take revenge, not to resist evil, and say "if any one strikes your right cheek, turn to him your left too."[51] Jesus did not resist those who persecuted him. He scolded Peter who tried to defend him. His death on the cross was the zenith of his non-violence and non-resistance.

The non-violence and the non-resistance of Jesus revealed the fact that God must be a non-violent, non-resistant God. This non-resistant God could never allow war at any time. For Christians to join military service is (a) to disobey God's will. To disobey God's will is to be violent. (b) It is to live a life against a non-violent - non-resistant God.

29.4. Because Jesus Taught Christians to be Non-Resistant

Christians should not join military service, because they are followers of Jesus. Jesus never told his disciples to join war. Instead, he told them not even to defend oneself against evil. He rather told them not to resist evil. He told them to allow people to persecute them.

29.5. Because Jesus Taught Christians to Love their Enemies

Christians should not join military service, because Jesus, their Lord, told them to love enemies. Those who join military service cannot love enemies, since they took oath to kill the enemies. Those who can love enemies can never join military service. Even if many Christians would say that the purpose of their joining military service is mainly to support the livelihood of the family, military service is contradicted to the teachings of Jesus.

29.6. Because Paul Taught Christians to Feed Hungry Enemies and to Give Water to the Thirsty Enemies

In the same way as Jesus taught the disciples to love the enemies, Paul told Christians to feed one's hungry enemies, and to give water to the thirsty enemies.[52] Paul must have given this advice to all those who accepted Christian Gospel. All Christians are supposed to be children of God. Therefore, it must be an advice to all Christians to love the enemies, and even feed them when they are hungry. Paul adviced Christians to put love into practice. John too said that love without action is not love. If the advice to love one's enemies is a good teaching, it is not right to teach Christians to join military services, because military services cannot always avoid war and killings.

29.7. Because Christians are Called to do Good But Not Commit Sin, Against Others

Christians are called to do good to others. They are not called to do harm to others. Therefore, Christians should not join military service, because military services often involves war. The golden rule suggests that Christians are supposed to be very good, doing good to others in the same way as we want others to do good to us. War is the opposite of this. In war, no one wants to do good to enemies. In war the aim is to destroy others as much as possible. It is due to presence of military service in every government that they used to fight war. Therefore, it is much better for Christians to avoid joining of military service.

Endnotes

49. Colossans 1:15.
50. John 14:9b.
51. Matthew 5:39.
52. Romans 12:20.

30

Christian Discipleship and Military Service

A Possible question to be asked among Christians is "Are all Christians disciples of Jesus or is there a special call for some Christians to be disciples of Jesus? The early Church seemed to regard every Christian as a disciple of Jesus. It is possibly true to say that all Christians are disciples of Jesus in the early Church. Today only about 30% percent Christians seemed to remain disciples of Jesus Christ, not because the rest of Christians are not called to be disciples, but because they cannot or do not want to live according to the standard of Christian discipleship. A study may reveal that many Christians joined military service as a result of their estrangement from true Christian discipleship. So, many Christians joined military service as they lost the footsteps of the non-violent non-resistant Lord, Jesus Christ. This may be shown clearly as follows:

(a) Imitation of Christ-for Christians as disciples of Christ, imitation of his life, his teachings, etc. is necessary and important. Apart from others, imitation of Christ includes imitation of his lowliness, his life for others, his love for his enemies, his non-violence, his non-resistance, etc are important. A disciple of Jesus is supposed to imitate Jesus' way of living for others. His care for the sick, the needy, the poor and the weak must be imitated. A Christian who lives for others cannot dedicate his life to kill others. This means that Christian life is in opposition to military service.

Moreover, since a true Christian is a disciple of Jesus, he/she is supposed to obey the teaching of Jesus to "love the enemies". So, if a

Christian loves his/her enemies, he/she is a true or good Christian. If a Christian is called to be the disciple of Jesus, he/she is also required to love his/her enemy. Therefore, Christian discipleship is contrary to military service and war. A Christian who joins military service is one who does not know about the way and will of Jesus Christ.

A Christian, as a disciple of Jesus, should also imitate his non-violence and his non-resistance. Non-violence and non-resistance may be a weapon of peace for Jesus. It may be used by him as a means to bring in peace in the world. St. Paul took the life of Jesus as an example to Christian life. He says: "Imitate me as I imitated Christ." While imitating every way of life of Jesus, here we particularize imitation of his non-violence and his non-resistance, as a means to extend the reign of God. Since Jesus is a non-violent, a non-resistant teacher, to wage war or to join military service is not only to stop following Jesus, but even to become his enemies. If we too choose to be non-violent - non-resistant, we could be true followers of Jesus. If we choose violence, we must become his enemies or traitors.

To be a disciple of Jesus is not so cheap. The difficulty of following Jesus may or may not be the same with the difficulty of rejecting military service. To remain a true disciple of Jesus Christ required Christians to reject the path of violence, and even the path of military service. No one who takes oath to follow the path of non-violence and non-resistance is admitted to the military service. Everyone who joins military service must take oath to use violence or arms. Therefore, one rightly or almost rightly says that anyone who decided to join military service decided to become the enemy of his Lord who is a non-violent - non-resistant Lord.

Jesus set an example of non-resistance not only in his life. He taught to follow the path of non-resistance when he says, "Do not resist evil doer", If anyone strikes your right cheek, turn to him your left too."[53] Jesus really wanted his disciples to be different from the world. While the world used violence, he wanted his disciples to use not only non violence, but even non-resistance.

There is much difference between non-violence and non-resistance. Non-violence can include avoidance of or rejecting arms, fighting with hands and knife, war, killings of any kind, etc. Non-resistance, on the other hand, goes much further. Non-resistance means allowing oneself to be persecuted more and more when someone has persecuted us. Jesus died on the Cross as a result of his use of non-resistance. However, through it, he rose again from the dead and became victorious. Jesus must have believed that if his disciples follow his non-resistance as a norm of life, they must win the world for God. Gandhiji too believed in non-violence as a means of victory. As such, India got Independence under his leadership.

Christians are supposed to learn this non-violence and non-resistance from his life and teachings. If Christians remain his followers they must also follow or imitate his non-resistance. Military service serves only as a means to become enemies of the non-resistant Christ. Christians may gradually understand the intention of Jesus.

Endnotes

53. Matthew 5:38

31

Right Approach to the Goal of Liberation

War is a wrong means to attempt to achieve liberation. It was a wrong way for Israelites to achieve liberation from Egypt by means of war. War is not a right means to reach lasting liberation. Israelites continue to have enmity with other nations because they used war in their international affairs. Therefore, they can never have lasting peace with other nations. This is because they used a wrong means of liberation. Equality is the goal of liberation. Equality with other people, socially, politically, economically, etc., is the true goal of liberation. Equality must be the original situation of human society too at the beginning before sin came into the world. It must be sin which caused social sins existed within human society. Social sins, Includes oppression, downtroddenness, exploitation, discrimination, marginalization, colonialization, male-chauvism, tyranny, injustice, caste practice, etc. These social sins rendered the weak and the poor socially captives for centuries. Such are the people who need liberation until they would become equal with the strong, the rich and the high castes.

In order to liberate such people gun-culture is a wrong means. Any kind of violence cannot do with the lasting liberation of this people. Bandhs and strikes cannot solve the problem of the weak and the helpless. Truth should be stated, truth should be practiced or lived. Truths condemning social evils should be effectively stated as the best means to liberate the oppressed, exploited, discriminated, etc. The problem is that tribals or backward people hardly speak of liberative truths.

It is too sinful to fight human beings. Fighting human beings is not a right approach to liberation or the goal of liberation. Fighting human beings is a sinful approach to liberation. It should not be used by Christians, because it is un-Christian.

If the word "fighting" cannot be avoided, what is to be fought is not human beings, but the evils practiced by such human beings. Dalit Theology is named as "Counter Culture."[54] Dalit Theology has to counter or fight caste practice and caste system as a whole, in India. If or when Dalit Theology would be victorious, caste practice would either be eliminated or left inactive. In the same way Asian Theology has fought past colonialism for many centuries in the past.[55] Asians would still continue to mention such past events in their theology until Asian countries reach the status or stature of developed western countries.

However, it is partly wrong to fight as such, as this approach appeared to be a fight against westerners. It should be fighting against wrong and harmful systems and evils as mentioned above. Still another way of saying the same thing is to say that to liberate the oppressed, truths must be stated. Truth is liberative, and if truth be stated it must work. Human problem is that truth always cannot be stated. Every bold speech is not always truth. Truths, which condemned social evils mentioned above, should be stated clearly, understandably, convincingly. A truth stated clearly is believed to liberate the poor and the oppressed.

Till the early part of the 20th century many Dalits were backward, illiterate, undressed, and were more like animals. At that time Brahmins in India treated them as if they were lower than animals.[53] However, tribals and dalits become educated, civilized, and semi-developed. Today Brahmins may no more oppress a dalit or tribal who got doctoral degrees in education. Dalits and tribals burst/ opened the shell of oppression, almost in the same way as an egg is burst out by a young chick when it is hatched.

However, we do not mean that one need to wait for civilization to liberate the poor and the oppressed. It must be wrong to wait for it to liberate them. Strong words on the equality of all human beings, and truths condemning social evils, such as tyranny, oppression, downtroddenness, marginalization, discrimination, injustice, alienation, etc. must be stated logically and authoritatively. Every one may agree that truths stated clearly and correctly must be understandable and acceptable to all. So, one of the best ways to achieve liberation is to eliminate social evils/sins.

Endnotes

54. M.E. Prabhakar, *A Reader in Dalit Theology*, ISPCK, New Delhi, 1988, pp. 3,4, 9-14.
55. Franklyn J. Balasundaram, *Contemporary Asian Christian Theology*, Delhi, ISPCK, Delhi, 1995, p. 1.

32

Means and Ways to Achieve Permanent Peace in the World

The past history of Israel shows that war never produce peace. Temporal victories never brought peace between the nations. It is known to all that Israelites used war as a means to deal with their neighbouring nations. They had a fight with every neighbouring nation. As a result of this, Israelites seems to have permanent enmity with Muslim nations around them. This historical fact partly proves that use of war in a nation's relation to other nations never keep permanent peace between the warring nations. A victory in war may keep temporal silence, as a result of the loser's draw-black or silence. However, it is not a peace; it is only a temporal silence as a result of fear of the victor. It may even be a silence with a preparation for future retaliation. The losers must be filled with anger and enmity, with a preparation for future war. The present world situation does not surpass this situation. This may partly prove that the world has nothing good, and it is filled with pessimists only. The world of war cannot produce bright optimism for a better future.

Even a super-power cannot keep a lasting peace in the world. A disobedient country may be suppressed by a super power. The suppression may produce a preparation for a bigger war, i.e., a star-war, on the part of the suppressed. In such a situation arms-race cannot be avoided. Arms-race should not be taken as an unavoidable part in the lives of human beings. It should be taken as an avoidable situation caused by an unnecessary use of arms against enemies. At least Christians should understand like this. Israelites are sleeping so long. Till today they are not awakened to realize the fact that it is due to their wrong view of God and his participation in war, that nations continue to wage war against each other. Israelites talked of Holy War. Muslims must have borrowed this idea from them. The whole world, including great nations too, seemed to take war, as if it is a natural part of the world order. In such a world enmity remains, like seeds, in the minds of every nation. In such a world there cannot be lasting peace.

Israelites must have a great show of repentance for this. They must show their repentance to the world for convincing the whole world that, war is a necessary part of human life. The result of this repentance would be the realization that war is a sin, that God never allowed war, that it is the Israelites who claimed that God leads Israelites in war, that God is captain of the army of Israel, warrior, etc. If and when Israelites have this great repentance, the world would come to realize the fact that it is the result of the Israelites view of war in the Old Testament that the whole world regarded war as necessary part of human life. Abolition of war and perfect hatred for war would be the result of Israelites' repentance for misguiding the world through the Bible. Abolition of war in the world would gradually bring in perfect hatred of war in the mind of people in the world.

Lasting peace in the world may began in the world only when gun-culture (and or arms-race) in the world is replaced by reconciliation, peace-pacts, love, brother-hood-sister-hood, neighbour-love, God's family, etc. As has already been discussed above, gun-culture in the world produced only arms race, or preparation for greater wars, or star war, enmity between nations. Abolition of gun culture is necessary to keep lasting peace in the world.

It is felt that Israelites, who have written the Old Testament, must initiate the work of reconciliation with its neighbouring nations as the initiative means to bring in lasting peace in the world. It is true to say that Christians read the Bible as the word of God. As such, in reading the Bible, they too believed that God really led Israelites in their wars against other nations. Since they believed the Bible as the word of God, they believed that God is warrior, captain of the army of Israel, etc. It is by depending on the Bible that they accepted war as a part of human life on earth. As such they used to fight war in the same way as Israelites used to do so.

Therefore, Israelites must initiate works of reconciliation with Muslim countries around them as a means to build up lasting or permanent peace in the world. That must be the beginning of lasting peace in the world. A wiser country should bow in front of other countries as a first step to initiate lasting peace in the world.

In order to establish a lasting peace in the world, the whole universe as the family of God must be enforced gradually. It is not far from the truth to say that the whole world is one family of God. And since truth can be understood by any rational being, everyone is believed to be able to understand this truth. If or when we can convince the whole world that the whole world is the family of God, feeling of enmity between nations would gradually vanish.

In such a situation brother-hood, sister-hood must grow in the lives of human beings. Brotherhood/sisterhood of all human beings must also be stressed strongly, even to convince people of the whole world. If all people in the whole world would be convinced that the world is one family of God and that all human beings are brothers and sisters lasting peace must become a fact in the world.

If the whole world realizes the fact that all human beings are brothers and sisters, love must readily become the means of global and national relationships. If there would be such a great love in the world "to love the enemy" must become possibility in the world. In the presence of love of the enemy "Neighbourly love", may become a lesser love in such a world of love. If the whole world is filled with individual love, neighbourly love, love of enemies etc., then there cannot be any war in such a world of love.

33

The Wisdom and Foolishness of Producing and Using Nuclear Bombs

Can God allow use of nuclear bombs in the world? We simply infer that God cannot allow use of nuclear bombs in the world. However, although we are to come back to the negative side, let us first discuss the possible positive views of nuclear arms.

33.1. The Wisdom of Producing Nuclear Bombs

It is not very important to discuss about the wisdom of producing Nuclear Bombs. The wisdom lies in the brain behind the production of the bombs. There is wisdom in the invention of any modern wonders. The scientist who invented any kind of the bombs must have extraordinary knowledge of science. He should be counted among one of the wisest men on earth. He should be one among great inventors of the modern age, such as inventors of aeroplane, television, video-film, mobile phone, computer/laptop, Vehicles, etc. Inventors of such inventions are makers of the modern age.

However, one should note the difference between inventor(s) of nuclear bomb and those of others. While other inventions can be used to facilitate life on earth, nuclear bombs are means to destroy life on earth.

It is believed that people who still have animal blood must welcome production of nuclear bombs. Many little children, too, could also admire the production of nuclear bombs. We have a strong hesitation to say that inventor's) of nuclear bombs is/are as wise as other inventors.

33.2. The Foolishness of Producing Nuclear Bombs

Although, we have just said that the inventor(s) of modern nuclear bombs is a wise man, we partly hesitated to praise him for this work. Because, wisdom does not always depend on the extraordinariness of what is done. Wisdom is also measured on the basis of the quality, goodness, etc. of the work done. A wicked fellow could hardly be called a wise man, even if he/she did some great achievements.

The inventor of nuclear bomb could somehow be called a foolish man. Because, he could or could not be much aware of the possible destructive results of his invention. He might have some interest and joy in the production. However, he may not have interest and joy in the possible destructions to be caused by his invention. If at all he has a chance to live again on earth, he may want to be swallowed by the crack of the earth. How could a man of sound mind think of producing such destructive weapon in God's world? It is a great foolishness to produce nuclear bombs under the Sun.

The work of producing nuclear bombs is a great foolishness; it could eventually mean a self-destruction.

33.3. The Foolishness of Using Nuclear Bombs

Use of nuclear bombs can be termed as a foolish work for the following reasons:

(a) That it is so much destructive

Use of nuclear bombs is foolishness, because it is so much destructive. It is understood in children's general knowledge that hydrogen bombs could be a hundred times more powerful than atom bombs dropped on the two cities of Hiroshima and Nagasaki of Japan, in the Second World War. Each atom bomb used in the Second World War were reported to destroy each city.

This means that a hydrogen bomb would be powerful enough to destroy a modern city with 10 to 15 million people. Use of 2000 such bombs within a minute may cause a strong earthquake much stronger than any earthquake before. Such a foolish act can destroy the whole surface of the earth even if the earth may not become dusts. Life on earth may partly or fully be destroyed.

Even in our tribal societies young people who are fighting each other become objects of ridicules. People began to regard such people as foolish people. In this context, people who try to harm others, people who try to destroy others are gradually taken as immature and foolish people. Those who still love to use nuclear bombs should now be regarded as foolish nations.

(b) That it can Instigate/Encourage Arms Race

Use of nuclear bombs can be termed as foolishness, as it can only encourage arms race. All the competitive countries may expect to become super powers in the future. The history of the world may turn to produce a new super power in the near future, as a result of use of nuclear bombs by today's power holders. This means that such a future would be the result of the foolishness of the powerful today. A Kuki proverb says "It is better to become wise earlier than later". It is better to eliminate nuclear weapons today than to see others use them against us.

(c) That it can encourage/instigate even terrorists and weaker countries to produce nuclear bombs

No one can say that terrorists could always be prevented from producing nuclear bombs. Terrorists could secretly send their scientists or inventors to learn to produce nuclear weapons. If no one uses such weapons, they may not easily be tempted to produce weapons. We all know that countries copy so many new inventions from the first country which produced such sophisticated weapons.

Therefore, those countries who first use nuclear bombs only taught other countries and even terrorists groups to learn from them. If terrorist groups would produce such weapons in future, then those countries who already produce such ones, would gradually realize that they taught them (terrorists or weaker countries) how to produce such weapons.

Therefore, we are right in saying that use of nuclear weapons is foolishness, because it is a way to produce or develop enemies who can use similar weapons.

(d) Because it is Unethical

Normal human beings who are in their right senses do not want to disturb others at work. Such people used to feel guilty to disturb others while sleeping at night or at any time. They do not like to disturb students reading their lessons. More than this is to live for others, to do something for the welfare of others, to do something to make others successful in whatever they do. It is to do good to all.

The opposite of this is to make plans to destroy others. Those who try to use weapons of mass destruction do not know what is ethical or what civic sense is. If it is wiser to avoid disturbing others at work, it is unethical to try to destroy others by means of weapons of mass destruction. Those who act un-ethically act foolishly. Those who produce and use nuclear bombs are not wise enough because they acted un-ethically.

(e) Because it is a Self-Destruction

Use of nuclear bombs would become a self destruction for the following reasons (1) Because all those living in the world are related to each other. (2) Because of social integrity (3). As Jesus says, "He who use sword will die of sword". (4). Because those who use such weapons are like a man who cut a branch on which he was sitting.

Use of weapons of mass destruction is an act of self destruction, and self destruction is foolishness. Therefore, we can see an act of foolishness in the use of nuclear bombs. This may be explained further in the following points. (1) Since all human beings living in the world have some relatedness. Everyone in the world is a part of us. Everyone is a part of one family of God, in which you and me too are a part of it. Therefore to destroy others by means of such weapons should mean destroying our parts. This may be clarified more by the next point. (2). Social integrity. It seems true to say that in any society there is a social integrity of everyone living in that society or community. Everyone living in it influence each other, and thus have partial relationship to each other. Even one's character or behaviour is more or less equal with that of others. In this context, if there are so many weak Christians in a community, others too cannot claim that they are spiritually strong and perfect. Because, a person is regarded as spiritually perfect only if and when he/she could influence the weak people of the society in one way or the other.

Almost in the same way, all human beings in the world has some relationships. To destroy others is to destroy our parts. True human beings would feel pain when they see that their fellow human beings are destroyed. Only true human beings have the true eyes to see the fact that when someone destroys fellow human beings, he/she is destroying himself/herself. Only those who can know this truth are true human beings. Those who would destroy others by means of nuclear weapons are destroying themselves. From this context, it is true to say that those who would destroy others by means of nuclear weapons, are destroying themselves. Therefore, those who destroy others, thus, are foolish people. There is madness in destroying others by means of weapons of mass destruction.

(f) Jesus Says "He Who use Sword will Perish by Sword"

There is a truth in saying that he who fought war will die of war, he who use sword will die of sword. He who uses nuclear weapons will perish by nuclear weapons. Therefore to use nuclear weapon must mean to destroy one-self. In this way we can prove that to use nuclear weapon to destroy others is foolishness because it is a self destruction. A men/woman who killed himself/herself too is regarded as an insane, or foolish, or one who has mental problem.

(g) Because it is Like a Man Who Felled a Branch on Which he was Sitting

Those who use nuclear weapons are like a man who climbed on a tree and felled the branch on which he was sitting. On the tree his life was depending on that branch. But he felled it, and destroyed himself. We live on earth. To use nuclear bombs to destroy others on earth is to destroy oneself, because we all are living on the same earth. To destroy the earth by means of nuclear weapons is to destroy life on earth. It is self destruction. Therefore, it is a real foolishness. The earth is life. To destroy the earth is madness. Without words, tribals in India could imagine the foolishness of increasing the number of nuclear bombs in the world, because, they too began to know that

2000 hydrogen bombs can destroy the whole surface of the earth in a single minute.

In our discussion on the wisdom and foolishness of the production and use of nuclear bombs, it is almost impossible to point out the wisdom of the work. Its foolishness over-weighed its wisdom so much that one can hardly mention its wisdom.

34

Wisdom will Bring an End to War and Nuclear Weapons

Any one in any religion may agree with the view that war is not a part of the original human life. It must be the result of sin ridden madness. War is not a work of wisdom. It must be started because of madness caused by sin. War itself seems to be a madness. Wise men in any country must agree with this view. Spare an hour or a day to think that war itself is a madness. Anyone who can spend a day to think as such, must finally agree to say that war is a madness. The same is with use of nuclear weapons. Use of nuclear weapons too is madness, as has already been discussed above.

Therefore, anyone can agree to say that wisdom can bring an end to war and use of nuclear weapons in future. It is possible to think that philosophers do not wage war. Philosophers used to think deeper. If they are asked to join war, they must think twice and finally avoid war. If this be true, then, it is true to say that those who think twice realize the madness of war and thus try to avoid war. Let us imagine that there is an Island of Philosophers. Philosophers alone lived in that Island. Since they are only philosophers, they cannot think of any war with any other nation. So, they decided not to wage any war. As such, they also decided not to manufacture any sophisticated weapons too. Thus, the island becomes a warless island.

This island of imagination is made to claim that wisdom can bring an end to war and weapons of mass destruction. An island of scientists may also be imagined as such. Scientists too may not like to wage war by their own hands. Let us claim that scientists too may want to reserve war for other groups of people-probably slaves of madness. If this be so, they do not want to wage war as they think of it as acts of madness.

It is possible to think that since war is fought by those who cannot think wisely, wisdom alone can bring an end to war. Now we suppose that after another millennium, all people in the world would become philosophers, scientists, sages, etc. Then they will realize the foolishness of war and use of nuclear bombs. At that time many may say, "How foolish were those people before us that they used to fight foolish wars?" They would become like Kukis today, who ask "How foolish and how wicked were we when we practiced head hunting in the past?" The fact is that when Kukis practiced head hunting before, they did not at all knew that head hunting was so wicked and so foolish. At that time they regarded head hunting as a part of their lives. But today they really realize the wickedness and foolishness of head hunting which they practice before.

The same thing will happen after the world would stop or abandon war. After the world would stop or abandon war totally, all will realize the wickedness and madness of war, and say like Kukis "How wicked and foolish were human beings before, that they used to fight each other in wars and destroy each other by using nuclear bombs?" When all people in the world would become wise in future, war would be looked back upon as a childish madness of the past. It may take so many years for human beings to become wise universally. The sooner all human beings become wise the earlier war will come to an end, and the later they become wise, the longer war would remain. In the same way, the sooner human beings know God in Isaiah's way, the sooner they would realize the foolishness of war, the later they know God in Isaiah's way, the longer war will continue in the world.

35

Gun-Culture will come to an end when Nations will be willing to Beat Swords into Plowshares and Spears into Pruning Hooks

Prophet Isaiah had foreseen perfect peace in the far future. Such a peace is to be produced by establishment of the kingdom of God. In his vision he fore-saw a future when nations will be willing to put down arms (weapons of all kinds) completely.

1. The Place of Swords and Spears in Wars in Ancient Times

Before guns were introduced in wars between ethnic groups and between nations in ancient times, swords and spears must be used as most important weapons of war. They must be more important weapons than bows and arrows. Therefore, prophet Isaiah must have mentioned them here in 2:4 as representatives of all weapons of war in ancient times.

2. When Nations will be willing to beat Swords and Spears into plowshares and pruning hooks

Since swords and spears could represent all weapons of war in ancient time, what prophet Isaiah must have meant would be that a day will come in future, when all nations would only like to turn weapons of war into house-hold instruments. Because, at that time nations will realize the evil of war. They will begin to see people of other nations as brothers and sisters, and as members in the same family. They will also begin to see God as Parent of all human beings. Their minds will become like that of a house wife who never think of a knife to be used to stab or kill someone. Such a house wife is said to have " No mind to kill." A killer used to think of a knife useful for killing someone. However, for a house-wife it is useful only for cutting vegetables in the kitchen. Prophet Isaiah must have fore-seen a time when nations will no more have the mind to kill or destroy other nations. At such a time there will be no space for storing weapons of war. Nations will only like to turn weapons of war into house-hold instruments like spade, kitchen-knife, pruning-hooks, plowshares, long daos for cutting grasses, etc., etc. What prophet Isaiah have fore-seen is total disarmament of all kinds of weapons of war including weapons of mass destruction. It will be time when spiritual eyes of nations will be opened to see the evil of war.

3. No Nation Shall lift Sword against other Nations

At such a time when everyone has only a "mind of peace", nations shall no more use weapons of war against any other nation. War should then be taken as an old sinful habit of the past. It should then be taken as "a past madness" traditionally taken down from generation to generation.

4. What kind of Changes would be there in the Life of Nations?

(a) There will be realization of madness of "Gun-culture, war, etc." It may be intellectual, mental, spiritual, religious, or any other awakening, which will make human beings realize that gun-culture is a madness inherited from madness of the past ages. This realization of war as a madness will make nations abandon gun-culture totally.

(b) Such a realization will be coincided with the realization that all human beings are brothers and sisters in a real family. It may take a long time for human beings to have a full realization of this. However, when such a thing would happen, it must really result into total abandonment of gun-culture and war. (c). This will also result into the realization of God as common Parent of all human beings and of the whole creation as well. Perfect realization of God as common Parent of all human beings and of the whole creation will be able to eliminate war in the universe.

(d) This kind of change will also completely remove enmity between nations in the world. Absence of enmity between nations will render weapons of war totally useless. Then there will be no more war between nations.

(e) In such a time, there will be universal fulfillment of the words of Jesus, "to love one's neighbour" and "to love the enemy." If and when nations love neighbouring countries and also love enemies, there will no more be war in the world.

(f) New and unbelievable kindness to others. At such a time nations will have new and unbelievable kindness towards others. This kind of kindness to others will make all aware of the evil of war, and therefore, no one will fight war anymore.

5. What will be the cause of such a great change in human history?

(a) Establishment of the Kingdom of God. Prophet Isaiah (2:1-5) said something about "the mountain of the Lord. Barry Webb claims that mountains played an important part in the religions of Israel's neighbours.[56] He claims that Isaiah has a vision of universal peace. He claims that the mountain of the Lord is a symbol of the coming kingdom of God, in which a purified and resurrected Zion is destined to play a crucial role.[57]

Let us suppose that the kind of perfect peace fore-seen by Isaiah is suppose to happen when the kingdom of God will be established. Again let us suppose that Jesus already established the kingdom of God predicted by prophet Isaiah. However, the problem is that, although the kingdom of God is already established by Jesus, the perfect peace fore-seen by Isaiah does not happen at all. Therefore, we have a tendency to ask another question, "Is the kingdom of God established by Jesus different from that kingdom of God fore-seen by prophet Isaiah?" The answer may not be whether the kingdom predicted by prophet Isaiah is different from or the same with that established by Jesus.

The effectiveness of the perfect peace predicted by Isaiah, as a result the establishment of the kingdom of God, is not depending on time. It is rather dependent on human response to the reign of God in human life. Barry Webb seems to be right in saying that Isaiah saw perfect peace to be ushered in the future, but asked his contemporaries to live in such a future now at present.[58] Let us suppose that Isaiah's request /urge for action was not responded well during his time. In the same way movement for peace is not in progress at present too. Therefore it is possible that Isaiah's urge for action in this regard is never fulfilled in human history, till today.

This also means that although Jesus established the kingdom of God, it does not automatically brought in perfect peace in the world.

What we want to emphasize is that prophet Isaiah must have believed that that perfect peace could be practiced or could have happened at any generation, if /when all human beings are in the position to accept Isaiah's suggestion for perfect peace. The kingdom of God or reign of God is also to be effective only in the actions or lives of human beings. This also means that the kingdom of God is meaningless unless it is made effective in the actions or the lives of human beings. Because, establishment of the kingdom of God is not like an erection of grave stones. It is to be made effective in the lives of believers. Although the kingdom of God mentioned by the prophet has been already established by Jesus, the perfect peace referred to by him has not come into force for two or more reasons. (i). Because Christians are of the opinion that such perfection cannot and will not happen during life on earth. Such a perfect life will happen only in heaven. (ii). Another way of understanding is that it will happen as a result of a sudden change or universal change. These two views must be taken as wrong views.

The true view must be that the arrival of prophet Isaiah's vision of perfect peace will come into force only when people are willing to allow God's reign in their lives. Perfect peace must be a product of right actions of believers as a result their true relationship with God.

(b) A similar answer to our question above is also to be found in prophet Isaiah's vision of the coming of that Davidic king called "a shot from the stump of Jesse" (11:1 – 9). According to this when he would come the earth will be filled with (a perfected) knowledge of God as water fills the sea." That kind of perfected knowledge will produce perfect peace between human beings and animals, and between animals and animals. At such a time total or universal disarmament will happen in the world. Here also we have the same problem. It is believed that that Davidic king has already come in the person of Jesus Christ. No Christian reject this view. This means that prophet Isaiah's vision has been fulfilled in the person of Jesus Christ. However, every Christian do agree that the peace predicted to be associated with the arrival or coming of that Davidic king, does not yet happened. The same thing should be said that the resultant perfect peace will not depend on time, nor will it wait for future in heaven. It should be the fruit of believers' true relationship to God. As Isaiah had asked his contemporaries to live in such a future at present, Christians are to live a life of such perfect peace. But not to wait for time and in heaven.

(c) Another belief is in prophet Jeremiah's view of the new covenant. According to prophet Jeremiah everyone will know God by himself/herself at that time. According to the writer of the letter to the Hebrews, the New Covenant has been already fulfilled in Jesus Christ. However, the kind of knowledge predicted by Jeremiah has not yet been in every believer. Therefore, we are to accept the view that what have been predicted by prophets must be fulfilled in the lives of human beings. Fulfillment of the predictions should not be watched in the future in miraculous happenings, or in time, in heaven.

In the same way as prophet Isaiah urged his contemporaries to live in the future at their own time (at their own present time), we are to emphasize urgent and complete abandonment of gun-culture or complete disarmament in the world today. We are to urge nations that perfect peace is the requirement of the world today. We are to tell the world not to wait for a sudden change in the world. Only by living in peace that the world will have peace. Our task today is to ask the world to actualize prophet Isaiah 's urge for complete abandonment of gun-culture in the world today.

In order to achieve this, gun-culture and war should be taken now as the last remains of ancient madness in human lives, and modern civilization still fails to realize its (war's) madness. It is an ancient darkness which modern light still fails to drive away. Even the Gospel is too weak to open the eyes of Christians to see the evil of gun-culture and or War.

Endnotes

56. ***The Message of Isaiah***, Leicester, 1996, p. 45, 46.
57. Cf. ***Ibid.***, pp.45, 46.
58. Cf. ***Ibid.,*** p.46.

Conclusion

The whole book tries to show the fact that although Israelites claimed that God used to involve himself in Israelites' war with other nations, it was Israelites who claimed as such. God really does not involve himself in war against other nations. It is like putting human words into the mouth of God.

Most of the men used by God in the Old Testament time either killed someone or involved themselves in wars. However, this involvement of men of God in war does not prove God's permission for war. Men of God like Abraham, Moses, Joshua, Judges, Kings etc. involved themselves in wars against other nations. However, their involvement in war does not prove that God allows war to be in the lives of his people. It only proved that men of God too had their weaknesses. Their involvement in war must be dark spots in their lives. It only meant that even men of God too have some sins in their lives. God accepted them because of their dedications. Their sins are forgiven, but their sins are not included among righteous acts.

This is stated to support the view that God never allows war. Designations given to God by writers of the Bible, such as warrior, captain of the army, etc. are not God's designations. They are human made designations for God. They are only examples of human beings made God in their own images. Human beings pictured God like themselves. Of course it is possible to describe God in human terms. But everyone knows that it is totally wrong to describe God as wicked human beings as drunkard, warrior, captain of the army, drug addicts, etc. To call God warrior is as good as and as bad as to call him drunkard. It is totally wrong to call God as warrior and captain of the army.

God is good to all. He is God of all nations. Therefore, one should not think of God as leading Israelites in their war with other nations. Moreover, Israelites need to realize the fact that God is parent of all human beings, and therefore God should not be thought of as enemy of other nations. Israelites must also be awakened to realize, that all human beings are brothers and sisters. They are supposed to love each other. They are not supposed to be enemies.

To know God rightly too means to maintain peace in the world. God is Creator of all and Saviour of all. He is non-violent-non-resistant God. This fact is shown by Jesus through His life and His teachings. Jesus Christ is the self-revelation of God. He shows us God's non-violence and God's non-resistance through His life and teachings. Christians should be perfect as their heavenly and earthly Parent is perfect.

By knowing all these, Christians should not even join military services as far as possible. By avoiding military services, Christians will have better chances to become true disciples of Jesus Christ. They may become more like their non-violent-non-resistant Lord. Christian life is a life of discipleship of Jesus. Discipleship includes imitation of Christ. To imitate the non-violence and the non-resistance of Christ is a very important part of imitation of Christ. To imitate His non-violence and His non-resistance does not mean to lose something. It is a means to be victorious. Jesus died on the Cross due to His non-resistance. However, through it he is victorious for eternity. He was raised again from the dead. War does not give permanent victory to anyone. Rather non-resistance is a means to be victorious. Christians should seek the way of non-violence and non-resistance, as a right way of victory, the right means to conquer the world for God.

It is almost impossible to achieve perfect peace today. Because, such a perfect peace as predicted by prophet Isaiah, cannot be achieved as a result of magical power, nor by an unexpected or sudden happening, nor by God's forceful interference.

Rather, in the same way as Isaiah had urged his contemporaries to live in such a future, it is to be achieved in the lives of believers. Only when believers really live in peace the beginning of perfect peace will slowly begin. So, believers are urged, today, to live in such a perfect peace without waiting for the future. Because what Isaiah have said about perfect peace will and can happen only in the lives of human beings. Therefore, it is wrong to ask a question, "When will this happen ?" Because, this will happen only in the actions and lives of believers or nations.

Bibliography

1. Balasundaram, Franklyn J., *Contemporary Asian Christian Technology*, ISPCK, Delhi, 1995.
2. Berkhof, Louis, *The History of Christian Doctrines*, Edinburgh, 1937.
3. Colin, C. "War", in *The International Dictionary of the New Testament*, Cumbria, 1986.
4. Dufour, XL, (Edit), *Dictionary of Biblical Theology*, Bangalore, 1967.
5. Flood, Govin, *An Introduction to Hinduism*, New Delhi, 1998.
6. Menninger, Carl, *Whatever Became of Sin*, New York, 1975.
7. Prabhakar, M.E., *A Reader in Dalit Theology*, ISPCK ,New Delhi, 1988.
8. Ralte, Lalrinmawii, *Femenist Hermeneutics*, IWTT, ISPCK, Delhi, 2002.
9. Richardson, Alan, *A Theological Workbook of the Bible*, London, 1988.
10. Webb, Barry, *The Message of Isaiah*, Inter-Varsity Press, Leicester, 1996.